THE
NORFOLK
POLL BOOK
1806

RAYMONDS ORIGINAL POLLBOOKS

Published by:
S.A. & M.J. Raymond,
6, Russet Avenue,
Exeter, EX1 3QB

ISBN: 1-899668-03-9

Produced for the Publishers by
Robert Boyd, Printing and Publishing Services,
260, Colwell Drive, Witney, Oxfordshire OX8 7LW

RAYMONDS ORIGINAL POLLBOOKS

Between 1696 and 1872, lists of voters in Parliamentary elections, indicating which candidate(s) they had voted for, were frequently published in the form of poll books. From 1832 onwards, electoral registers listing persons entitled to vote were also regularly published. Other information was also frequently included in poll books: addresses, or, at least parishes of residence, were usually given; sometimes a distinction was made between resident and out-voters; occupations were sometimes stated. Arrangement was very variable: some grouped voters by parish, ward, or even street; others provided a straightforward alphabetical listing; a few listed them by trade, or in the order in which votes were cast. There is little uniformity in the way in which information is presented; furthermore, whilst pollbooks for many elections survive for some constituencies, for others there are none. There is, for example, no published poll book for the counties of Cornwall or Somerset, although a few survive in manuscript.

Despite all these vagaries, poll books and electoral registers, where they survive, are extremely valuable sources of information for local historians and genealogists. In those constituencies where the franchise was wide, they frequently list thousands of people, and are invaluable in assisting the local historian to reconstitute the historical community, or enabling the genealogist to identify the homes of particular families. The Westminster pollbook of 1774, for example, lists over 7000 voters, giving their residences and occupations. It is a key source for the occupational history of the capital, quite apart from its value to the genealogist.

Unfortunately, it is rare for more than a few copies of particular poll-books to survive, and only a handful have been reprinted in recent years. Access to the information contained in them is therefore very restricted. The aim of **Raymond's Original Pollbooks** is to make them much more widely available in facsimile.

Since this series consists of facsimiles, the quality of printing may, in some instances, leave something to be desired. A facsimile reprint can only be as good as the source from which it is taken - and paper has many enemies. Consequently, in some volumes there may well be evidence of fading, of print seeping through the paper to come out on the other side, of pages that have been badly cut or damaged, etc. Such imperfections are inevitable, and it is better to save what remains by reprinting, than to insist on perfection, and consequently deprive the historian of access to an important source.

It should be noted that many pollbooks, in addition to lists of voters, also include candidates' speeches, squibs, and other electoral proceedings. In general, these are not reproduced in this series.

This is not the place to give a detailed account of pollbooks. If you require more information on their availability and use, you should consult the following:

GIBSON, JEREMY & ROGERS, COLIN. *Poll books, c.1696-1872: A directory to holdings in Great Britan.* 4th ed. Federation of Family History Societies, 1994.

SIMS, J. *A handlist of British Parliamentary poll books.* University of Leicester History Dept. Occasional publication 4. 1984.

VINCENT, J.R. *Pollbooks: how Victorians voted.* Cambridge University Press, 1968.

THE POLL

FOR

KNIGHTS OF THE SHIRE

FOR THE

COUNTY OF NORFOLK,

OPENED

ON THURSDAY, THE THIRTEENTH OF NOVEMBER,

AND CLOSED

ON *WEDNESDAY, THE NINETEENTH,*

1806.

⸺⸺⸺⟨◍⟩⸺⸺⸺

HENRY LEE WARNER, ESQ. HIGH-SHERIFF.

𝕮𝖆𝖓𝖉𝖎𝖉𝖆𝖙𝖊𝖘.

	VOTES.
The Right Hon. *William Windham, of Felbrigg,* ..	3722
Thomas William Coke, Esq. of Holkham, ...	4118
The Honorable *J. Wodehouse, of Witton Park,* ..	3365

NORWICH:

PRINTED AND SOLD BY R. M. BACON, AND MAY BE HAD
OF ALL OTHER BOOKSELLERS.

THE
NORFOLK POLL,

OF 1806.

	Win.	Coke	Wod.

Acle.

BOULT George, gent. Acle
Bunton James, watch-maker, ditto
Clarke John, bricklayer, Hindringham
Curtis John, carrier, Acle
Dawson William, cowleech, Loddon
Evans William, cordwainer, Acle
Felmingham William, sen. bricklayer, ditto
Hurrell James, farmer, ditto
Leath John, surgeon, ditto
Riches Francis, farmer, ditto
Riches Henry Jolly, ditto, ditto
Russell Robert, blacksmith, ditto
Sayer John, baker, ditto
Shingles Thomas, maltster, ditto
Shepherd William, gent. Freethorpe
Smith John, glazier, Acle
Wilkins William, husbandman, ditto

	Win.	Coke	Wod.
	10	10	8

Alburgh.

Aggas John, farmer, Alburgh
Barwick Isaac, ditto, ditto
Butcher John, ditto, ditto
Burgess John, ditto, ditto
Catling James, gent. ditto
Crowe John, farmer, ditto
Dawson John, ditto, Denton
Denny John, ditto, Wortwell
Edwards James, ditto, Alburgh
Gower James, ditto, Alburgh and Wortwell

	Win.	Coke	Wod.

Alburgh.

Harvey Robert, jun. farmer, Wortwell
Kett David, labourer, Redenhall
Kerr James, gent. ditto
Meeke John, farmer, Alburgh
Moore Henry, tailor, ditto
Pedgrift John, mason, ditto
Smith Samuel, cordwainer, ditto
Turner Robert, gent. ditto

	Win.	Coke	Wod.
	9	12	8

Alby.

Carr John, yeoman, Alby
Franklin William, cordwainer, Hackford

	Win.	Coke	Wod.
	2	1	1

Aldeby.

Bacon Robert, yeoman, Aldborough
Beckett James, farmer, Aldeby
Boult Benjamin, ditto, Yarmouth
Bowler Robert, gardener, Aldeby
Burroughs Peter, gent. ditto
Chalker James, farmer, ditto
Dyke Thomas, carrier, Erpingham
Fairweather John, farmer, Aldeby
Huke William, ditto, ditto
Needham John, cordwainer, ditto
Rising John, farmer, Toft Monks
Tripp John, cordwainer, Aldeby
Utten Philip, farmer, ditto
Wragg John, ditto, Burgh St. Peter

	Win.	Coke	Wod.
	3	3	11

Aldborough.

Aldhouse John, grocer, Aldborough
Cubitt John, yeoman, Saxthorpe
Gambling John, ditto, Aldborough
Gay John, esq. ditto
Lubbock James, gardener, Aldborough
Woodcock James, surgeon, ditto

	Win.	Coke	Wod.
	5	4	2

Alderford.

Porrett Robert, farmer, Alderford

	Win.	Coke	Wod.
	1	1	0

Alpington.

	Win.	Coke	Wod.
Cutling John, farmer, Alpington			
Nichols Peter, ditto, ditto	2	2	0

Alethorpe.

	Win.	Coke	Wod.
Riches Robert, farmer, Field Dalling	1	1	0

Anmer.

	Win.	Coke	Wod.
Coldham James, esq. Anmer	0	1	1

Antingham.

	Win.	Coke	Wod.
Helsden Benjamin, yeoman, Gimmingham			
Powell John, blacksmith, Antingham			
Sutton Stephen, farmer, North Walsham	0	0	3

Ashby with Oby.

	Win.	Coke	Wod.
Harnard William, jun. farmer, Thurne	0	0	1

Ashby.

	Win.	Coke	Wod.
King Robert, miller, Ashby			
Marshall Zaccheus, farmer, ditto			
Woolsey Jeremiah, ditto, ditto	2	3	1

Ashill.

	Win.	Coke	Wod.
Jary Roger, farmer, Marham			
Jerry Robert, ditto, Ashill			
Leggett John, ditto, ditto			
Mallows Robert, ditto, ditto			
Mallows Robert, ditto, ditto			
Miller Robert, ditto, Hempstead			
Oldfield Henry, ditto, Ashill			
Stebbing John, labourer, North Pickenham			
Thompson James, carpenter, Ashill			
Towler John, farmer, Gooderstone			
Tompson John, carpenter, Ashill			
Watts John, Stanhoe, clerk, ditto	8	11	4

Ashmanhaugh.

	Win.	Coke	Wod.
Dawson Thomas, thatcher, Tunstead			
Grout John, collar-maker, Ashmanhaugh			
Popay William, tailor, ditto	0	0	3

Ashwelthorpe.

	Win.	Coke	Wod.
Barker Robert, labourer, Ashwelthorpe			
Colman William, farmer, ditto			
Harvey Thomas, ditto, Wymondham			
Huggins Wm. watch-maker, Ashwelthorpe			
Utting Thomas, farmer, ditto	1	2	3

Ashwicken.

	Win.	Coke	Wod.
Herring William, farmer, Middleton	1	1	0

Aslacton.

	Win.	Coke	Wod.
Alden John, labourer, Aslacton			
Arnold Roger, husbandman, ditto			
Lincoln James, farmer, ditto			
Long John, ditto, ditto			
Milligan John, cordwainer, ditto			
Read John, farmer, ditto			
Utting Richard, gent. ditto			
Woodcroft John, husbandman, ditto			

Attleborough.

	Win.	Coke	Wod.
Barnard Robert, farmer, Attleborough			
Barnabas Burrows, ditto, ditto			
Beck John, surgeon, ditto			
Blumpton William, glazier, ditto			
Brighton John, higler, ditto			
Carver John, farmer, ditto			
Chapman Jonas, labourer, ditto			
Chapman James, ditto, ditto			
Cowles Richard, ditto, ditto			
Chapman William, carpenter, ditto			
Colman William, farmer, ditto			
Copping Samuel, gent. Rockland St. Andrew			
Coe Wm. Rippin, farmer, Attleborough			
Dodd Thomas, miller, ditto			
Fielding John, victualler, Rockland All-Sts.			
Fiddy Robert, butcher, Attleborough			
Francis Richard, watch-maker, ditto			
Francklin Fairfax Rev. clerk, ditto			
Green William, victualler, ditto	1	1	7
Handsworth William, farmer, ditto			
Harmer William, miller, ditto			
Harper John, labourer, Hingham			

Attleborough.

Name	Win.	Coke	Wod.
Hill Charles, labourer, Attleborough			
Hovill James, farmer, ditto			
Howes John, ditto, ditto			
Kiddell Robert, cordwainer, ditto			
Kerrison Thomas, bricklayer, ditto			
Kiddell Wm. Cann, grocer, ditto			
Knights John, farmer, Carleton Rode			
King Charles, blacksmith, Attleborough			
Lindoe John, carpenter, ditto			
Littleproud William, farmer, ditto			
Littleproud Thomas, ditto, ditto			
Lock Jonathan, ditto, Great Ellingham			
Michael Mariner, surgeon, Attleborough			
Parson William, auctioneer, ditto			
Page William, cordwainer, ditto			
Page John, labourer, Shropham			
Parke Francis, farmer, Attleborough			
Philips John, carpenter, ditto			
Plumpton Nathaniel, blacksmith, ditto			
Rainer Daniel, farmer, ditto			
Rose James, ditto, ditto			
Saysane Robert, labourer, ditto			
Warren Nathaniel, weaver, ditto			
Whitley Thomas, labourer, ditto			
Wright Robert, farmer, ditto			
	34	26	21

Aylsham.

Name	Win.	Coke	Wod.
Ashley Stephen, wine-merchant, Skeyton			
Barham William, yeoman, Holt			
Canfor Robert, basket-maker, Briningham			
Colver J. B. clerk, Hackford			
Copeman Robert, gent. Foulsham			
Copeman Peter, draper, Kerdiston			
Dotheredge Wm. collar-maker, Newton St. F.			
Drake Thomas, gent. Aylsham			
Fish John, gent. Matlaske			
Francis Robert, grocer, Marsham			
Hogge Joseph, gent. Wormegay			
Howard Dennis, farmer, Burnham Norton			
Johnson Benjamin, millwright, Beighton			
Peterson John, yeoman, Aylsham			
Plane Edward, ditto, ditto			

Aylsham.

Name	Win.	Coke	Wod.
Powell William, gent. Banningham			
Rackham Baker, ditto, Brandiston			
Repton William, ditto, Sloley			
Roofe William, baker, Felmingham			
Scottow Edmund, yeoman, Barningham			
Taylor Copeman, farmer, Gunthorpe			
Waller John, yeoman, Southrepps			
	9	10	13

Aylmerton.

Name	Win.	Coke	Wod.
Clarke Charles, yeoman, Aylmerton			
Paul John, ditto, ditto			
	2	2	0

Baconsthorpe.

Name	Win.	Coke	Wod.
Girdlestone Rev. Theop. clerk, Baconsthorpe			
Springall Joseph, yeoman, S. Erpingham			
Spurrell John, ditto, Baconsthorpe			
Warnes John, ditto, ditto			
Wilson Peter, farmer, Smallburgh			
	1	1	4

Bacton.

Name	Win.	Coke	Wod.
Atkinson Henry, clerk, Bacton			
Baldwin Thomas, farmer, Worstead			
Clarke William, ditto, Bacton			
Colk John, ditto, ditto			
Denham Robert, bricklayer, ditto			
Maris Thomas, farmer, ditto			
Rump Thomas, yeoman, ditto			
Shepherd John, jun. farmer, Bacton			
Watling John, merchant, Dickleburgh			
	3	3	6

Bagthorpe.

Name	Win.	Coke	Wod.
Morse John, esq. Bagthorpe			
Somers John, publican, East Rudham			
	1	2	1

Bale.

Name	Win.	Coke	Wod.
Barnsdall Matthew, gardener, Bale			
Beresford Robert, carrier, ditto			
Burcham John, land-surveyor, Cawston			
Gutteridge John, farmer, Bale			
Long William, yeoman, ditto			
Long William, farmer, ditto			
Long Matthew, worstead-weaver, ditto			
	7	7	0

Column headings: Win. | Coke | Wod.

Banham.

Bailey Charles, carpenter, Banham
Betts John, farmer, ditto
Calver Robert, ditto, ditto
Chapman William, labourer, ditto
Cracknell William, farmer, ditto
Cunningham Jonathan, ditto, ditto
Edwards John, ditto, ditto
Estling William, ditto, ditto
Fox Nicholas, cordwainer, ditto
Gayner Robert, farmer, ditto
Gilbert Robert, millwright, ditto
Hewitt William, farmer, Old Buckenham
Humfrey Francis, ditto, Banham
Hunt John, ditto, Old Buckenham
Hubbard Thomas, yeoman, Banham
Jessup Jonathan, bricklayer, ditto
Jolly John, farmer, ditto
Ludkin Henry, carpenter, ditto
Morley James, farmer, Winfarthing
Murrell Richard, ditto, Banham
Page Thomas, ditto, ditto
Palmer Richard, ditto, ditto
Philips Robert, farmer, Banham
Philips Pulleyn, ditto, Old Buckenham
Potter Ames, ditto, New ditto
Shaw William, ditto, Banham
Smith Daniel, carpenter, ditto
Syder Thomas, gent. ditto
Taylor John, bricklayer, ditto
Taylor Samuel, farmer, Old Buckenham
Watson William, thatcher, Banham
Weston John, farmer, ditto
Woods Robert, gent. ditto

(totals: 16 | 21 | 19)

Banningham.

Barnes Edward, yeoman, Banningham
Bradford John, farmer, Yarmouth
Drosier John, yeoman, Roughton
Elden William, ditto, Erpingham
Mack Robert, ditto, Banningham
Marsh Jeremiah, ditto, ditto

Column headings: Win. | Coke | Wod.

Banningham.

Page John, yeoman, Banningham
Scott John, cordwainer, ditto

(totals: 1 | 1 | 7)

Barford.

Allen William, turner, Barford
Bultitaft Neave, husbandman, ditto
Clarke Thomas, ditto, ditto
Girdlestone Ishmael, farmer, ditto
Leeder John, ditto, Little Melton
Lightwing Samuel, cordwainer, Barford
Nash Samuel, farmer, ditto
Smithson Robert, blacksmith, ditto
Webster Samuel, farmer, ditto

(totals: 6 | 7 | 3)

Barney.

Bond John, shopkeeper, Palling
King James, farmer, Holt
Porter Robert, ditto, Barney
Wilson Andrews, ditto, ditto
Winn Israel, gent. Wells
Wright John, publican, Thursford

(totals: 4 | 5 | 2)

Barnham Broom.

Childs John, farmer, Barnham Broom
Childs Thomas, husbandman, ditto
Childs William, blacksmith, ditto
Harley Richard, husbandman, ditto
Howlett Riches, carpenter, Hardingham
Jary Richard, miller, Barnham Broom
Liddelow William, farmer, Barnham Broom
Press Edward, clerk, Old Buckenham
Smithson Wm. blacksmith, Barnham Broom
Turner Andrew, carpenter, ditto

(totals: 0 | 0 | 10)

Barningham Town.

Ellis Samuel, yeoman, Guestwick
Gibbs William, ditto, Little Barningham
Twiss Francis, farmer, Felthorpe

(totals: 1 | 1 | 2)

Barningham Parva.

	Win.	Coke	Wod.
Barns John, farmer, Briston			
Ellis William, yeoman, Little Barningham			
Overton William, shepherd, Barningham			

Barningham Norwood.

	Win.	Coke	Wod.
...eak Robert, yeoman, Gresham			
...artridge Robert, ditto, Bassingham	2	3	1

Barton Bendish.

	Win.	Coke	Wod.
Eblen Thomas, surgeon, Brooke			
Flood Robert, cutler, Barton	2	1	0

Barton Turf.

	Win.	Coke	Wod.
Bacon Joshua, farmer, Barton Turf			
King Augustine, ditto, ditto			
Morse John South, esq. Yarmouth			
Nockolds William, farmer, Barton Turf	2	2	0

Barwick.

	Win.	Coke	Wod.
Hoste William, esq. Barwick	1	0	4

Basham East.

	Win.	Coke	Wod.
Astley Rev. H. N. clerk, Foulsham			
Sands James, carpenter, Thornage	1	1	0

Basham West.

	Win.	Coke	Wod.
Baldrey Charles Morley, esq. West Basham			
Brett Thomas jun. farmer, Burnham Overy	0	2	1

Basham North.

	Win.	Coke	Wod.
Dowsing Horatio, clerk, North Basham	2	2	0

Bassingham.

	Win.	Coke	Wod.
Butterfield John, labourer, Bassingham			
Frankland George, yeoman, ditto			
Spurrell John, ditto, ditto	1	1	0

Batcburgh.

	Win.	Coke	Wod.
Bailey William, labourer, Bawburgh			
Darby James, farmer, Great Melton			
...de William, innkeeper, Bawburgh			
Hart Thomas, farmer, ditto	3	3	0

B

Brœburgh.

	Win.	Coke	Wod.
Head Hart, wheelwright, Bawburgh			
Norton Benjamin, esq. ditto	5	6	1

Brodestvell.

	Win.	Coke	Wod.
Buckenham Henry, gardener, Bawdeswell			
Catton William, wheelwright, Shipdham			
Curson John, farmer, Bawdeswell			
Fish John, husbandman, ditto			
Fisher William, shopkeeper, Holt			
Lloyd Richard, esq. Bawdeswell			
Margerson John, farmer, ditto			
Moulton Stephen, grocer, ditto			
Neal John, farmer, ditto			
Sly Thomas, shoe-maker, ditto			
Smith William, farmer, ditto			
Stonex Benjamin, wheelwright, ditto			
Stone Henry, cordwainer, ditto			
Tann Thomas, farmer, ditto			
Trory William, bricklayer, ditto			
Wymer Richard, carpenter, ditto	13	14	3

Brœsey.

	Win.	Coke	Wod.
Marsters Thomas, jun. farmer, Wormegay	1	1	0

Bayfield.

	Win.	Coke	Wod.
Jodrell Henry, esq. Bayfield	0	0	1

Beckham West.

	Win.	Coke	Wod.
Emery Benjamin, yeoman, West Beckham			
Flower Samuel, ditto, ditto			
Sayers James, ditto, ditto	2	2	1

Bedingham.

	Win.	Coke	Wod.
Foulger Robert, farmer, Bedingham			
Hudson Nicholas, miller, ditto			
Plaford Robert, farmer, Loddon			
Stone George, esq. Bedingham	2	2	2

Beechamwell.

	Win.	Coke	Wod.
Motteux John, esq. Beechamwell			
Smith James, farmer, Ashill	2	2	0

Beeston.

	Win.	Coke	Wod.
Allison John, farmer, Whissonset			
Barnes Thomas, farmer, Halvergate			
Beare Jonathan, husbandman, Beeston			
Clarke Benjamin, farmer, ditto			
Davy John, farmer, ditto			
Dearns Robert, cooper, ditto			
Gilding True, farmer, ditto			
Leath Edward, ditto, Great Fransham			
Payne Wm. publican, North Tuddenham			
Shickle Robert, husbandman, Gt. Fransham			
Tuck John, carrier, Litcham			
Wright Thomas, husbandman, Tittleshall	6	8	7

Beeston St. Andrew.

	Win.	Coke	Wod.
Micklethwayt Nathaniel, esq. Hickling	1	1	0

Beeston St. Lawrence.

	Win.	Coke	Wod.
Cubitt Benjamin, farmer, Halvergate	0.	1	1

Beeston Regis.

	Win.	Coke	Wod.
Cocks John, fisherman, Sherringham			
Cremer Cremer, esq. Beeston Regis			
Ward Joseph, yeoman, ditto			
West Edmund, fisherman, Sherringham			
Wilkinson Benjamin, esq. Thornage			
Woolrow Cremer, gent. Runton	6	5	0

Beetley.

	Win.	Coke	Wod.
Duffield Robert, farmer, Whissonset			
Miller Robert, ditto, Yaxham			
Rayner Edward, ditto, Beetley			
Reeve Daniel, gent. ditto	1	1	3

Beighton.

	Win.	Coke	Wod.
Ames James, farmer, Pulham St. Mary			
Fowler Richard, ditto, Brighton			
Fowler Samuel, ditto, ditto			
Hewitt Samuel, ditto, Hasingham			
High Thomas, ditto, Brighton			
Howard Robert, ditto, ditto			
Littlewood James, ditto, ditto			
Thurketle Richard, labourer, Hasingham	7	7	1

Belaugh.—South Erpingham.

	Win.	Coke	Wod.
Allen Thomas, labourer, Belaugh			
Allen James, ditto, ditto			
Chaplin Edward, yeoman, ditto			
Hagon William, ditto, ditto			
Worts Robert, ditto, Mundesley	1	1	4

Belaugh.

	Win.	Coke	Wod.
Archer Robert, farmer, Ingham			
Blomfield William, farmer, Carbrook			
Johnson William, gent. Beeston			
Warnes James, farmer, Hindringham	3	3	1

Bergh Apton.

	Win.	Coke	Wod.
Batchelor William, gent. Chedgrave			
Beevor Augustus, clerk, Bergh Apton			
Cooke Thomas, gent. ditto			
Harvey John, farmer, Yarmouth			
Haywood John, ditto, Bergh Apton			
Mayes James, ditto, ditto			
Rushmore Charles, ditto, ditto	3	5	3

Besthorpe.

	Win.	Coke	Wod.
Bales John, labourer, Attleborough			
Bishop Simon, farmer, Morley St. Peter			
Buckenham Daniel, ditto, King's Lynn			
Howes Abraham, ditto, Besthorpe			
Johnson John, ditto, ditto			
Leeder Robert, husbandman, South Lopham			
Page James, farmer, Besthorpe			
Page John, ditto, ditto			
Rose James, ditto, Hingham			
Warren James, ditto, Besthorpe	3	3	8

Bexwell.

	Win.	Coke	Wod.
Drew James, gent. Downham Market			
Sole Robert, clerk, Bexwell	1	1	1

Billingford.—Earsham Hundred.

	Win.	Coke	Wod.
Drake Francis, farmer, Billingford	0	0	1

Billingford.

	Win.	Coke	Wod.
Bromfield William, shepherd, Billingford			
Blomfield James, farmer, ditto			
Good William, wheelwright, Swanton Morley			
Hipkin John, carpenter, Billingford			
Hart Robert, farmer, Dillington			
Millet Jonathan, blacksmith, Elsing			
Spooner George, yeoman, Billingford			
Whiteman Thomas, farmer, ditto	8	8	0

Billockby.

Christmas John, farmer, Clippesby	0	0	1

Bilney East.

Allison William, husbandman, East Bilney			
Chambers William, farmer, ditto	2	2	0

Binham.

Booty James, Yalloway, farmer, Beeston			
Booty John, ditto, Blakeney			
Langham Richard, ditto, Hindringham			
Lox William, ditto, ditto			
Simpson Simon, gent. Wells	5	5	0

Bintry.

Goald Nathaniel, carpenter, Bintry			
Maystone Samuel, farmer, ditto			
Sawyer John, blacksmith, ditto			
Watts Robert, farmer, Hackford	4	4	0

Bircham Great.

Higcane Thos. farmer, Shouldham-Thorpe			
Holland Edm. farmer, Wiggenhall St. Mary			
Knowles William, publican, Burnham Ulph	2	3	1

Bircham Little.

Coxford James, blacksmith, Bircham Tofts	1	1	0

Birley.

Storey John, farmer, Bixley	1	1	0

Blakeney.

Barrett Richard, yeoman, Blakeney			
Bond Thomas, merchant, ditto			

Blakeney.

	Win.	Coke	Wod.
Brereton Robert, merchant, Blakeney			
Drewell John, mariner, Stiffkey			
Dunn Thomas, yeoman, Blakeney			
Jackson William, bricklayer, ditto			
Johnson Thomas, merchant, ditto			
Morgan Robert, blacksmith, ditto			
Shepherd James, cordwainer, ditto			
Taylor John, gent. ditto			
Temple Thomas William, merchant, ditto			
White John, mariner, Stiffkey	5	9	7

Blickling.

Bates John, gardener, Stoley			
Harbord the Hon. W. A. Blickling			
Hunt James Holley. esq. Burgh			
Walker Matthew, yeoman. Blickling			
Wicks William, gent. Colby	0	2	5

Blofield.

Bane Matthew, publican, Blofield			
Barker James, carpenter, ditto			
Bulley Charles, cordwainer, ditto			
Culley Benjamin, surgeon, ditto			
Davy William, husbandman, ditto			
Dunt Adam, tailor, Acle			
Elliot Thomas, gent. South Walsham			
England George, shoe-maker, Acle			
Grimble James, husbandman, Blofield			
Harrison William, farmer, Acle			
Horner William, publican, Blofield			
Howard John, farmer, ditto			
Massey Thomas, gent. Hemblington			
Matthews John, farmer, Blofield			
Morey John, carpenter, Acle			
Overed James, farmer, Blofield			
Postle Davy, ditto, ditto			
Rope Charles, ditto, Halvergate			
Saul Thomas, ditto, South Burlingham			
Sanderson James, gardener, Blofield			
Smith Joshua, glazier, Acle			
Simmons Philip, gardener, Blofield			
Tann John, miller, ditto			

	Win.	Coke	Wod.

Blofield.
Tunear John, sawyer, Blofield
Tuck Samuel, farmer, ditto

	Win.	Coke	Wod.
	17	19	7

Blo Norton.
Andrews Thomas, farmer, Blo Norton
Browne Charles, clerk, ditto
Corble Joseph, farmer, ditto
Firmin John, ditto, ditto
Fordham Robert, miller, ditto
Fordham Thomas, farmer, ditto
Land William, ditto, Garboldisham
Nunn Edmund, ditto, Blo Norton
Payne John, linen-weaver, ditto
Scarie James, farmer, ditto
Smith Francis, ditto, ditto
Turner James, ditto, ditto
Walker Thomas, ditto, ditto

Bodham.
Clarke John, farmer, Bodham
Deriley Robert, ditto, ditto
Frankling Henry, ditto, ditto
Fuller John, cordwainer, ditto
Wegg George, yeoman, Foulsham

	Win.	Coke	Wod.
	2	3	11

Booton.
Lloyd Richard, farmer, Hardingham

	Win.	Coke	Wod.
	0	0	5

Boughton.
Carter Thomas, farmer, Denver
Reeve Richard, ditto, Boughton
Steward Samuel, ditto, Wereham

	Win.	Coke	Wod.
	1	1	0

Bracon Ash.
Berney Thomas Trench, esq. Bracon Ash
Corbould John, clerk, Bracon Ash
Green Robert, farmer, Hapton
Howard James, carpenter, Coltishall
Sewell John, gent. Mulbarton

	Win.	Coke	Wod.
	0	0	3

Bradenham East.
Wiggett John, farmer, Great Ellingham

	Win.	Coke	Wod.
	1	2	4
	0	0	1

	Win.	Coke	Wod.

Bradenham West.
Bentham James, clk. West Bradenham
Payne Jonathan, farmer, ditto
Reader William, bricklayer, ditto
Trendle Forby, farmer, ditto
Wells William, cooper, ditto
Watts Robert, farmer, ditto

	Win.	Coke	Wod.
	1	1	6

Bradfield.
Cale William, labourer, Southrepps
Collins John, yeoman, Knapton
Sidney Thomas, ditto, Bradfield
Waterson John, gent. ditto

	Win.	Coke	Wod.
	0	0	4

Bradiston.
Deere John, gent. Bradiston
Present William, butcher, Yarmouth
Stanford Jon. husbandman, Strumpshaw

	Win.	Coke	Wod.
	1	1	2

Bramerton.
Hennall John, schoolmaster, Kirby Bedon
Rudd Robert Gray, farmer, Bramerton

	Win.	Coke	Wod.
	1	1	1

Brampton.
Threadwell John, paper-maker, Brampton

	Win.	Coke	Wod.
	1	1	0

Brancaster.
Bellamy George, farmer, Burnham Westgate
Bolton William, clerk, Brancaster
Clarke Edward, grocer, ditto
Holsworth Robert, smith, ditto
Norton Francis, farmer, ditto
Simms Law, gent. ditto
Tennant Mark, farmer, ditto

	Win.	Coke	Wod.
	6	6	1

Brandiston.
Atthill John, yeoman, Cawston
Riches William, farmer, Brandiston

	Win.	Coke	Wod.
	2	2	0

Brandon Parva.
Bennett John, labourer, Little Brand
Bretnall George, linen-weaver, Feltwell
Briggs James, husbandman, Little Brand

Brandon Parva.

	Win.	Coke	Wod.
Batch J. R. esq. Great Cressingham			
Coleman James, farmer, Hilgay			
Dobbs William, ditto, Little Brand			
Garwood Samuel, ditto, ditto			
Goward Francis, husbandman, ditto			
Randall William, brickburner, ditto			
Sutton John, farmer, ditto			
Sutton William, ditto, Barnham Broom			
Willett Field, banker, Feltwell			
Wright Robert, farmer, Marlingford			

Breccles.

	Win.	Coke	Wod.
Margram Mark, farmer, Stowbedon	6	7	7

Bridgham.

	Win.	Coke	Wod.
Dunham Charles, esq. Bridgham	0	0	1

Briningham.

	Win.	Coke	Wod.
Binton Edward, farmer, Briningham			
Colman John, bricklayer, ditto			
Locksmith Robert, farmer, ditto			
Waller R. G. ditto, ditto	0	0	1

Brinton.

	Win.	Coke	Wod.
Baker John, labourer, Little Snoring			
Brereton John, grocer, Brinton			
Brereton Abel, gent. ditto			
Shirley Francis, draper, Stanhoe	2	2	2

Brisley.

	Win.	Coke	Wod.
Bensley William, farmer, Brisley			
Brookes Philip, grocer, King's Lynn			
Frohawk Francis, farmer, Brisley			
Gerrard Thomas, ditto, East Bilney			
Johnsons John, ditto, Beeston			
Mitchell James, husbandman, Brisley			
Mason Henry, farmer, ditto			
Mott Charles, publican, ditto			
Walter Weavor, clerk, ditto	4	4	0
Ward James, farmer, East Bilney	5	6	5

Bressingham.

	Win.	Coke	Wod.
Bryant Edward, linen-weaver, Bressingham			
Burrell William, gent. Roydon			
Chasteney Thomas, miller, Bressingham			
Cock Thomas, linen-weaver, ditto			
Davy John, farmer, Scole			
Deve John, ditto, Bressingham			
Ellis Robert, ditto, Shelfanger			
Houghton William, gent. Diss			
Martin Robert, esq. Bressingham			
Noble Thomas, husbandman, ditto			
Potter Robert, farmer, ditto			
Robinson Thomas, ditto, ditto			
Read Ezekial, ditto, South Lopham			
Read John, ditto, Bressingham			
Roper John, ditto, ditto			
Smith Thomas, linen-weaver, ditto			
Whitbread Robert, ditto, ditto	6	10	12

Briston.

	Win.	Coke	Wod.
Carr John, farmer, Briston			
Canham Jacob, blacksmith, ditto			
Crofts John, farmer, Hindringham			
Dean Thomas, ditto, Briston			
Drake James, publican, ditto			
Emery John, farmer, ditto			
Goddard John, ditto, ditto			
Greeves William, school-master, ditto			
Hill Joseph, farmer, ditto			
Hall Robert, innkeeper, ditto			
Jarmy Richard, yeoman, ditto			
Norris William, baker, ditto			
Parke Joshua, carpenter, ditto			
Pinnock Thomas, farmer, ditto			
Sacheverel John, husbandman, ditto			
Sharpens Thomas, farmer, ditto			
Spicer Charles, gent. ditto			
Spencer Robert, farmer, ditto			
Weston William, baker, ditto			
Williamson Thomas, farmer, ditto			
Woodcock Thomas, grocer, ditto	19	17	4

c

Brockdish.

	Win.	Cole	Wod.
Aldous John, blacksmith, Brockdish			
Booty William, jobber, ditto			
Burgess John, wheelwright, ditto			
Burgess James, farmer, Needham			
Carter John, husbandman, Brockdish			
Chilver Joseph, breeches-maker, Brockdish			
Colman John, farmer, ditto			
Doughty John, ditto, ditto			
Fisk Thomas, labourer, ditto			
Gibbs Lawrence, clerk, ditto			
Rayner Robert, carpenter, ditto			
Reeve Henry, butcher, ditto			
Safford Samuel, gent. ditto			
Wright Thomas, farmer, ditto	1	5	13

Broome.

	Win.	Cole	Wod.
Bird James, farmer, Broome			
Cooke Stephen, gent. South Lopham			
Day Jeremiah, gent. Broome			
Gibbon William, bricklayer, ditto			
Smith Richard, wheelwright, Scole			
Smith Robert, carpenter, Broome	5	4	2

Brooke.

	Win.	Cole	Wod.
Bailey Robert, gent. Surlingham			
Butcher Robert, farmer, Brooke			
Castell William, clerk, Brooke			
Fryer Richard farmer, Brooke			
Hinsby Henry, ditto, Barford			
Norton Sam. farmer, Stratton St. Michael	3	3	4

Brundall.

	Win.	Cole	Wod.
Harper Henry, husbandman, Brundall	0	0	1

Brunstead.

	Win.	Cole	Wod.
Burton Nathaniel, dealer, Brunstead			
Chaddick William, yeoman, ditto			
Cubitt Samuel, farmer, ditto			
Durrant William, ditto, Honingham	0	0	4

Buckenham.—Blofield Hundred.

	Win.	Cole	Wod.
Green John, farmer, Beighton	2	2	0
Johnson Russell, farmer, Burgh			

Buckenham New.

Aldis William, carpenter, New Buckenham			
Bevor Thomas, esq. Wilby			
Brighton John, labourer, New Buckenham			
Cary William, butcher, ditto			
Catermoul Thomas, baker, ditto			
Davey Edward, farmer, Attleburgh			
Dodd John, surgeon, New Buckenham			
Doubleday Martin, labourer, ditto			
France John, clerk, Old ditto			
Fromow John, weaver, New ditto			
Fulcher Thomas, gent. ditto			
Gall John, farmer, ditto			
Goss William, carpenter, ditto			
Gunton Joseph, chandler, ditto			
Haylett John, sadler, ditto			
Hewitt James, farmer, Old ditto			
Holl Samuel, cordwainer, New ditto			
Johnson Samuel, glazier, ditto			
Orford James, weaver, ditto			
Orford William, carrier, ditto			
Raynes William Burton, currier, ditto			
Reynolds Thomas, shopkeeper, ditto			
Rudderham John, bricklayer, ditto			
Rudderham Joseph, ditto, ditto			
Smith Robert, weaver, ditto			
Sword Benjamin, gent. ditto			
Sparling Robert, bricklayer, ditto			
Stebbing Thomas, ditto, ditto			
Townsend Thomas, sadler, ditto			
Jownsend John, tanner, ditto			
Wallis Seth, whitesmith, ditto			
Whitehead William, weaver, Hingham			

Buckenham Old.

	Win.	Cole	Wod.
Algar Robert, gent. Old Buckenham			
Baxter Joseph, higler, ditto			
Betts Charles, farmer, ditto			
Betts William, ditto, ditto	22	16	19

Buckenham Old.

Bowles John, farmer, Old Buckenham
Ellis John, ditto, Old ditto
Foulsham James, ditto, New ditto
Fulcher William, carpenter, Old ditto
Gedge George, farmer, ditto
Hayward William, ditto, ditto
Herbert George, gent. ditto
Hewitt John, farmer, New ditto
Kyburn Robert, ditto, Old ditto
Larter Robert, ditto, ditto
Last John, ditto, ditto
Lanmer John, ditto, ditto
Lucas Joseph, school-master, ditto
Marsh John, farmer, ditto
Norton Henry, ditto, Attleburgh
Norton William, ditto, Great Ellingham
Palmer Robert, ditto, Old Buckenham
Palmer Robert, carpenter, Banham
Potter Robert, farmer, South Lopham
Potter Daniel, higler, Old Buckenham
Quantrell Joseph, ditto, ditto
Randall William, gent. ditto
Roper Robert, farmer, ditto
Rush Marlborough, ditto, ditto
Scales William, ditto, ditto
Smith Robert, ditto, ditto
Snelling Thomas, ditto, ditto
Turner Earsham, ditto, ditto
Walker Samuel, tailor, ditto
Winfield James, farmer, ditto

Bunwell.

Austin Isaac, farmer, Bunwell
Ayton Robert, ditto,
Bale Edward, ditto, Wicklewood
Barker George, ditto, Bunwell
Chesteney William, ditto, ditto
Hardiman Thomas, ditto, Wymondham
Hardiman Robert, ditto, Bunwell
Hardy William, ditto, ditto
Long James, ditto, ditto
Long William, ditto, ditto

Win.	Coke	Wod.
27	24	9

Bunwell.

Ludkin Henry, farmer, Bunwell
Parsons William, ditto, ditto
Tyte John, labourer, ditto

Burlingham North.

Beevor John, clerk, North Burlingham
Heath Thomas, farmer, South Walsham
Jary William, esq. North Burlingham
Litlewood James, husbandman, ditto
Miles Thomas, farmer, Hasingham
Rope Robert, ditto, Halvergate
Smith John, ditto, Blofield

Win.	Coke	Wod.
0	11	13

Burlingham South.

Futter Robert, husbandman, Beighton
Heath William, farmer, Lingwood

Win.	Coke	Wod.
3	4	4

Burgh St. Peter.—Clavering Hund.

Boon William, sen. farmer, Burgh St. Peter
Boon William, jun. ditto, ditto
Boycett William, clerk, ditto
Chettleburgh Thomas, farmer, ditto
Disney Robert, ditto, ditto
Ellis Peter, ditto, ditto
Jones John, ditto, ditto
Smith William, labourer, ditto

Win.	Coke	Wod.
2	2	0

Burgh.—South Erpingham Hund.

Burr Edmund, yeoman, Burgh
Jones William, ditto, Skeyton
Parmeter Robert, merchant, Aylsham
Woolsey John, jun. yeoman, Erpingham

Win.	Coke	Wod.
0	1	8

Burgh.—Flegg Hundred.

Allared John, farmer, Burgh
Cobb John, carpenter, Rollesby
Copping William, farmer, Burgh
Dyball Robert, carpenter, ditto
Durrant Robert, miller, ditto
Dyball John, farmer, ditto
Dyball John, labourer, ditto

Win.	Coke	Wod.
1	3	2

Burgh.—Flegg Hundred.

	Win.	Coke	Wod.
Dyball Thomas, carpenter, Burgh			
Fabb John, farmer, Hemsby			
Fisher William, esq. Yarmouth			
Florence Thomas, ditto, Burgh			
Homan Edward, farmer, ditto			
Monsey Thomas, farmer, ditto			
Pettinghall Harber, butcher, Martham			
Woodrow John, husbandman, Burgh			
Woodrow John, ditto, ditto	7	7	10

Burnham Thorpe.

Balls John, farmer, Sharrington			
Everett Daniel, clerk. Burnham Thorpe			
Humphreys Philip, miller, ditto			
Ives Theophilus, farmer, Southrepps			
Woodbine Wm. smith, Burnham Thorpe	5	4	1

Burnham Westgate.

Bellamy W m. miller, Burnham Westgate			
Brown Thomas, farmer, Burnham Ulph			
Brett Thomas, sen. gent. ditto Overy			
Cremer Francis, surgeon, ditto Westgate			
Crowe Henry, clerk, ditto Depdale			
Dolman John, cooper, ditto Westgate			
Francis Richard, gent. ditto			
Glasse John, clerk, ditto			
Hancock John, labourer, ditto Ulph			
Matthews Barn. watch-maker, do. Westgate			
Messingham Wm. gent. ditto			
Osborn Butcher, farmer, Alburgh			
Simms Law, grocer, Burnham Westgate			
Tenant Matthew, tailor, ditto			
Walker Robert, bricklayer, ditto			
Weatherhead William, attorney, Blo Norton	15	15	1

Burnham Ulph and Sutton.

Ellis John, gent. Burnham Ulph			
Johnson Richard, smith, ditto Westgate			
Williamson John, ditto Ulph	3	3	0

Burnham Overy.

Beeston Thomas, miller, Burnham Overy			
Brett William, farmer, ditto			

Burnham Overy.

	Win.	Coke	Wod.
Cook Dennis, miller, Burnham Overy			
Cooke Richard, ditto, ditto			
Dennis J. cordwainer, ditto			
Foulger John, farmer, ditto			
Green William, tailor, Briston			
Groome James, farrier, Burnham Overy			
Groome James, jun. stone-mason, ditto			
Middleton Matthew, mariner, ditto			
Redhead William, farmer, ditto			
Savory Edmund, miller, ditto			
Tooley William, gardener, ditto	13	13	0

Burnham Norton.

Alby John, warrener, Briston			
Bird Isaac, mariner, Blo Norton			
Fuller Samuel, cordwainer, Burnham Norton			
Leaky John, mariner, Wells			
Oakes John, farmer, Burnham Norton			
Smith William, mariner, Blo Norton			
Smith Thomas, cordwainer, ditto	7	7	0

Burnham Depdale.

Overman Robert, farmer, Burnham Depdale	1	1	0

Burston.

Beale Timothy, farmer, Burston			
Carter Robert, ditto, ditto			
Dixon William, ditto, ditto			
Ellis William, yeoman, ditto			
Horne John, farmer, ditto			
Hunt John, surgeon, ditto			
Knowles John, farmer, ditto			
Self Robert, ditto, ditto			
Spurling William, ditto, ditto			

Buxton.

Barnham James, gent. Besthorpe			
Bewbridge John, yeoman, Buxton			
Frankling Thomas, gent. ditto			
Hayne Michael, carpenter, Marsham			
Jewell William, clerk, Swanton Abbotts	8	9	1

Calthorpe.

Horner Francis, cooper, Calthorpe
Saame Henry, yeoman, Aylsham

Cantley.

Curtis Richard, husbandman, Cantley
Gilbert William Henry, farmer, ditto
Morris James, ditto, ditto
Shanke William, gent. ditto
Shuckford Isaac, farmer, Halvergate

	Win.	Coke	Wod.
	4	4	0

Carbrooke.

Alpe Robert, farmer, Gressenhall
Gilman Charles Case, ditto, Hingham
Howard Joseph, gent. South Burgh
Lusher John, farmer, Carbrooke
Murrell Jehosaphat, ditto, ditto
Robinson William Lane, gent. ditto
Stone David, miller, ditto
Stone Roger, farmer, ditto
Tollman John, labourer, ditto
Trumpess Thomas, gent. ditto
Whitby William, farmer, ditto
Worby John, ditto, ditto

	Win.	Coke	Wod.
	4	4	1

Carlton.

Hopwood Richard, husbandman, Carlton
Perkins Francis, farmer, Surlingham

	Win.	Coke	Wod.
	2	1	1t

Carlton East.

Blackwood Wm. husbandman, East Carlton
Cannell Samuel, gent. ditto
Traxton Richard, husbandman, ditto
Traxton Thomas, gardener, ditto

	Win.	Coke	Wod.
	2	2	0

Carlton Forehoe.

Neve William, farmer, Deopham

Carlton Rode.

Adcock Thomas, farmer, Stratton St. Mary
Browne Thomas, ditto, Carlton Rode
Browne Zach. ditto, ditto
Browne William, ditto, ditto

	Win.	Coke	Wod.
	0	0	4
	0	0	1

Buxton.

Rump Richard, yeoman, Lammas
Symonds Robert, ditto, Buxton
Tuck John, labourer, ditto
Watts Alexander, yeoman, ditto

Caister, by Norwich.

Brewerton Thomas, farmer, Caister St. Edm.
Everett George, ditto, Forncet St. Peter
Warren William, ditto, Fritton

	Win.	Coke	Wod.
	5	5	5

Caister, by Yarmouth.

Bitton William, miller, Caister
Branford William, farmer, ditto
Burton Clement, husbandman, ditto
Clowes Thomas, gent. ditto
Carpenter William, farmer, ditto
Cowells John, blacksmith, ditto
Crane William, shoe-maker, ditto
Church John, farmer, ditto
Crane Thomas, husbandman, ditto
Daniel Thomas Reeve, farmer, ditto
Edmunds Joseph, husbandman, ditto
Edmunds James, cordwainer, ditto
Frazier John, tanner, Yarmouth
Green Daniel, husbandman, Caister
Kerridge William, gardener, ditto
Kittle Joseph, husbandman, ditto
Mayes John, farmer, ditto
Pettingall Robert, ditto, ditto
Symonds Joseph, carpenter, ditto
Symonds John, gardener, ditto
Tubby Robert, husbandman, ditto
Ward Henry, bricklayer, ditto
Waters John, spinner, Yarmouth

	Win.	Coke	Wod.
	1	2	2
	23	23	0

Caldecot.

Browne Thomas, labourer, Hindringham

Calthorpe.

Earl James, yeoman, Calthorpe
Elden John, blacksmith, Gresham

	Win.	Coke	Wod.
	0	0	1

D

Carlton Rode.

	Win.	Coke	Wood.
Briggs Elisha, farmer, Carlton Rode			
Buxton John, clerk, ditto			
Cornell John, farmer, ditto			
Cornell John, jun. ditto, ditto			
Fisher Samuel, gent. ditto			
Glover James, farmer, ditto			
Hardy Robert, ditto, ditto			
Haystead John, ditto, ditto			
Holl Edward, victualler, New Buckenham			
Kemp Richard, farmer, Carlton Rode			
Kemp Robert, ditto, ditto			
Lewell Thomas, ditto, ditto			
Ollett Daniel, ditto, ditto			
Page Thomas, ditto, Wymondham			
Rush John, ditto, New Buckenham			
Self John, ditto, Bunwell	6	12	15

Castleacre.

	Win.	Coke	Wood.
Balls William, carpenter, Castleacre			
Barton Thomas, farmer, Rougham			
Dewing Thomas, farmer, Swaffham			
Dodman James, glover, Castleacre			
Gooch William, baker, ditto			
Hill John, schoolmaster, Watlington			
Martin William, merchant, Castleacre			
Palmer Stephen, tailor, Stoke			
Priest S. J. miller, Castleacre			
Smith William, labourer, Docking			
Ward Abel, farmer, Hempton			
Wiscard Nicholas, thatcher, Sporle			
Winchfield Abel, fellmonger, Castleacre	13	13	0

Castle Rising.

	Win.	Coke	Wood.
Fawsett William, esq. Walpole St. Peter			
Lewis John, paper-maker, West Newton			
Wakefield James, yeoman, Castle Rising	1	2	2

Caston.

	Win.	Coke	Wood.
Alderton John, cooper, Caston			
Barker Benjamin, clerk, ditto			
Beaumont George, farmer, ditto			
Egliseton John, blacksmith, Stow Bedon			

D 2

Caston.

	Win.	Coke	Wood.
Forster Henry, blacksmith, Caston			
Gooch Samuel, weaver, ditto			
Grigson William, clerk, ditto			
Hardy John, farmer, ditto			
Hardy Robert, ditto, ditto			
Parslee John, farmer, ditto	7	2	6

Catfield.

	Win.	Coke	Wood.
Amis John, esq. Catfield			
Barton George, farmer, ditto			
Crowe James, ditto, Ludham			
Crowe William, ditto, Catfield			
Cubit George, esq. ditto			
Davey Samuel, yeoman, ditto			
Greensmith John, farmer, Hickling			
Hammond Thomas, ditto, ditto			
Knights Benjamin, butcher, Catfield			
Rogers Laurence, farmer, ditto			
Wells Nicholas, ditto, Hickling	4	5	7

Catton.

	Win.	Coke	Wood.
Bulwer Edward, clerk, Guestwick			
Clark James, wheelwright, Wereham			
Dixon Owen, smith, Foxley			
Harvey Thomas, esq. Catton			
Ives Jeremiah, ditto, ditto			
Ives Jeremiah Harvey, esq. ditto			
Rant Richard, farmer, ditto			
Sewell Joseph, gent. ditto			

Cawston.

	Win.	Coke	Wood.
Austin Matthew, butcher, Cawston			
Baker Richard, D. D. ditto			
Brett Benjamin, wheelwright, Bawdeswell			
Grout Robert, yeoman, Cawston			
Hill Francis, gent. ditto			
Lambert Robert, carpenter, ditto			
Newman John, gent. Hevingham			
Pammell Peter, ditto, Cawston			
Partridge William, yeoman, ditto			
Page Edward, ditto, ditto			
Plune John, shopkeeper, ditto	7	7	1

Cawston.

	Win.	Coke	Wod.
Rainbird Phillip, surgeon, Starston			
Robertson Henry, yeoman, Cawston			
Robertson John, gent. ditto			
Robins William, yeoman, ditto			
Robins William, miller, ditto			
Smith Thomas, yeoman. ditto			
Simpson William, Cawston	13	18	8
Tawell Martin, yeoman, ditto			
Taddenham Thomas, cordwainer, ditto			
Wilson James, bricklayer, ditto			

Chedgrave.

	Win.	Coke	Wod.
Barnard V. L. clerk, Stockton			
Branch Robert, bricklayer, Chedgrave			
Crisp John, farmer, ditto	4	4	3
Crisp Anthony, bricklayer, ditto			
Ellis Clement, tailor, ditto			
Gilbert Henry, gent. Loddon			

Choseley.

	Win.	Coke	Wod.
Willis Thomas, farmer, Brancaster	1	1	0

Claxton.

	Win.	Coke	Wod.
Pinor Charles, farmer, Claxton	1	1	0

Clenchwarton.

	Win.	Coke	Wod.
Catling John, farmer, Clenchwarton			
Fish Thomas, ditto, ditto			
Longbottom James, gent. ditto			
Pond Edward, cordwainer, ditto			
Rogers Robert, farmer, ditto			
Steward Thomas, ditto, ditto			
Sutterby Jonathan, ditto, ditto			
Wardale John, ditto, ditto			

Cley.

	Win.	Coke	Wod.
Hunt Holley Edm. gent. Ersingham			
Jackson Thomas, merchant, Blakeney			
Johnson William, tanner, Cley	7	6	2
Smith John, gent. Pulham St. Mary			
Thurston Robert, farmer, Holt			

Cley.

	Win.	Coke	Wod.
Thomlinson John Winn, esq. Cley	6	7	0
Walker Samuel, carpenter, ditto			

Clippesby.

	Win.	Coke	Wod.
Pollard John, farmer, Martham	1	1	0

Cockley Cley.

	Win.	Coke	Wod.
Crowe James, farmer, Holme Hale			
Crowe Thomas, ditto, Foulden			
Dashwood J. R. esq. Merkshall	0	4	5
Dashwood Horatio, clk. Caister St. Edmund			
Nursebox John, wheelwright, Cockley Cley			

Colby.

	Win.	Coke	Wod.
Caleby Rev. George, clerk, Colby			
Roper Snelling, yeoman, ditto			
Roper S. D. ditto, ditto			
Sharpling Robert, ditto, ditto			
Shepherd Samuel, ditto, Banningham			
Wright Robert, labourer, Colby			

Colkirk.

	Win.	Coke	Wod.
Burton Walter, smith, Hempton Green			
Goggs Robert, farmer, Horningtoft			
Harpley James, gent. Litcham	2	2	4
Kendle Thomas, labourer, Wells			
Savory Samuel, gent. Bintry			
Utber Thomas, farmer, Oxwick			

Colney.

	Win.	Coke	Wod.
Gibson William, clerk, Colney	4	6	2
Postle Jehosaphat, esq. Hetherset			

Coltishall.

	Win.	Coke	Wod.
Ansell Robert, plumber, Coltishall			
Bendy C. Wm. surgeon, Burnham Westgate			
Broome George, merchant, Coltishall			
Brown Robert, ditto, ditto	1	1	1
Burton John, blacksmith, ditto			
Church Joseph, clerk, Mattishall			
Church Thomas, surgeon, Coltishall			

Win. | Coke | Wood.

Coltishall.

Cole Richard, yeoman, Coltishall
Doughty Thomas, ditto, Belaugh
Hawes Siday, brewer, Coltishall
Neve Thomas, carpenter, ditto
Palgrave William, esq. merchant, ditto
Palgrave Thomas, ditto, ditto
Perkins Henry, gent. ditto

5 | 8 | 10

Colton.

Daveney Henry, esq. Colton
Ottaway Robert, husbandman, ditto
Uting John, farmer, Wramplingham

0 | 0 | 3

Congham.

Elsden Henry, esq. Congham
Lincoln William, yeoman, Stow
Palmer John, farmer, Congham
Riches James, miller, Grimstone

3 | 3 | 1

Corpusty.

Goldsmith Thomas, farmer, Wood-dalling
Harvey Richard, yeoman, Itteringham
Johnson John, farmer, Foxley
Johnson Henry, ditto, Barney
Wagstaffe Robert, publican, Briston

4 | 4 | 1

Costessey.

Garwood William, shopkeeper, Thetford
Hastings William, carpenter, Costessey
Hastings Edward, yeoman, Ringland
Hastings Francis, gardener, ditto
Pettitt Francis, farmer, Drayton
Sadler John, husbandman, Costessey
Savage John, gardener, Drayton
Sursham James, carpenter, Attleborough

7 | 7 | 1

Cranwich.

Partridge Rev. John, clerk, Cranwich

0 | 0 | 1

Cranworth.

Clarke Francis, farmer, Granworth
Crompton Thomas, clerk, ditto

Win. | Coke | Wood.

Cranworth.

Littleproud James, miller, Cranworth
Long David, farmer, ditto

0 | 2 | 4

Creak North.

Cork Robert, cordwainer, North Creak
Hendry Robert, wool-comber, ditto
Herod Thomas, farmer, ditto
Tilson Robert, ditto, ditto

4 | 4 | 0

Creak South.

Bembridge George, yeoman, Stody
Benstead James, labourer, South Creak
Daniels William, shepherd, South Creak
Elmer Michael, farmer, ditto
Graver Thomas Lombe, ditto, Attlebridge
Graver George C. ditto, Hindolveston
Holmes Jeremiah, bricklayer, South Creak
Hubbard John, ditto, ditto
Lack George, thatcher, ditto
Leamon Philip, grocer, ditto
Feverington Roger, labourer, ditto
Martin Thomas, ditto, ditto
Morley John, cordwainer, Mundham
Morley John, farmer, South Creak
Oliver John, sadler, ditto
Seppings Thomas, farmer, ditto
Shackcloth William, miller, ditto
Shackcloth Thomas, shepherd, ditto
Thurlow Giles, farmer, ditto
Turner Davy, farmer, ditto
Turner Davy, jun. ditto, ditto
Turner Charles, gent. ditto
Wacey Thomas, cordwainer, ditto

21 | 22 | 2

Cressingham Great.

Alderson Robert, farmer, Great Cressingham
Browne Edward, ditto, ditto
Buck Henry, blacksmith, ditto
Codling William, gent. ditto
Edwards Rev. Andrew, clerk, ditto
Spinks Benjamin, cordwainer, ditto-

0 | 0 | 6

Cressingham Little.

	Win.	Coke	Wod.
Clermont Wm. Chas. Viscount, L.Cressing.			
Dorr Thomas, farmer, ditto			
Norman Thomas, miller, ditto			
Pratt John, thatcher, ditto	4	4	0

Crimplesham.

Roberts Henry, yeoman, Crimplesham			
Royle William, clerk, Tilney cum Islington	1	1	1

Cringleford.

Ewen John, farmer, Cringleford			
Leeke William, miller, Corpusty			
Smyth John, esq. Topcroft	1	1	2

Cromer.

Curtis James, blacksmith, Cromer			
Custance William, mariner, ditto			
Jarvis William, mariner, ditto			
Leak Benjamin, shoemaker, ditto			
Neale Jonathan, cordwainer, ditto			
Peele Edmund, tailor, ditto			
Pearson Francis, sen. draper, ditto			
Ransome Sherman, mariner, ditto			
Ransome Henry, ditto, ditto			
Rust Benjamin, draper, ditto			
Sanford Henry, merchant, ditto			
Sexton Allen, fisherman, ditto			
Smith William, carpenter, ditto			
Tucker George Cook, publican, ditto			
Turner Samuel, miller, ditto			
Wardlaw Henry, yeoman, ditto			
Webb Robert, carpenter, ditto			
Wyndham George, esq. ditto			
Witting John, innkeeper, Gresham	18	15	1

Crostwick.—Tunstead Hundred.

Shepherd Martin, farmer, Crostwick	0	0	1

Crownthorpe.

Bunn John, farmer, Wymondham	0	0	1

E

Croxton.—Grimshoe Hundred.

	Win.	Coke	Wod.
Bidwell Woodward, farmer, Croxton			
Draper James, labourer, Thursford	0	1	1

Darsingham.

Chadwick George, farmer, Darsingham			
Clarke John, wheelwright, ditto			
Culham Hamond, gent. ditto			
Hamond Philip, esq. South Wootton			
Hawes Edward, yeoman, Darsingham			
Sharp Henry, farmer, ditto			
Shildrake Francis, cordwainer, Hunstanton			
Smith John, farmer, Darsingham			
Smith William, miller, ditto			
Smith William, gent. ditto			
Smith Thomas, blacksmith, ditto			
Sturley John, ditto, Leziate			
Stanton William, farmer, Darsingham			
Stanton Richard, ditto. ditto			
Watson William, ditto, ditto	9	10	7

Dalling Field.

Brooks James, farmer. Field-dalling			
Boyce John, ditto. ditto			
Brown Daniel, gent. Fulmodeston			
Coe John, farmer. Holt			
Coe John, ditto, Field-dalling			
Loose Andrew, ditto, ditto			
Spaul John, cordwainer, ditto			
Walker George, farmer, ditto			

Dalling Wood.

Breese James, yeoman, Wood-dalling			
Burton John, bricklayer, ditto			
Bulwer Thomas, farmer, ditto			
Eke William, ditto, ditto			
Godwin Hall, ditto, ditto			
Ives Robert, ditto, ditto			
Pegg Joseph, thatcher, ditto			
Reynolds Joseph, labourer, ditto			
Vout Charles, carpenter, Salt			
Wodehouse Anthony, sen. Wood-dalling	6	7	3
	7	7	3

Wm. Coke | Wood.

Deopham.

Babcock Edmund, smith, Deopham
Childerhouse Robert, husbandman, ditto
Clarke Robert, farmer, ditto
Cunningham John, labourer, ditto
Dey Jonathan, farmer, ditto
Dobbs John, ditto, ditto
Easton Isaac, ditto, ditto
Fenix Taylor, thatcher, Hackford
Frances John, farmer, Deopham
Jolly John, ditto, ditto
Jolly Richard, ditto, ditto
Jolly William, ditto, ditto
Knights Robert, ditto, ditto
Reeve John, ditto, ditto
Rowing Archibald, ditto, Morley St. Botolph
Sparkhall Isaac, ditto, Deopham
Sparkhall Timothy, ditto, ditto
Sparkhall James, ditto, ditto
Taylor Ganett, ditto, Attleburgh
Taylor Stephen, ditto, Deopham

Denver.

Beeton William, farmer, Denver
Blower Thomas, yeoman, ditto
Brook Robert, victualler, ditto
Clarke Zachariah, farmer, Hilgay
Collingwood William, victualler, Denver
Curson Edward, farmer, ditto
Dade Charles R. clerk, ditto
Dering J. Thurlow, esq. ditto
Flatt John, farmer, ditto
Hopkin John, ditto, ditto
Hopkin William, ditto, ditto
Hudson John, cooper, ditto
Lock John, ditto, ditto
Mann Rev. Charles, clerk, Oulton
Manfield John, yeoman, Denver
Palmer Thomas, shoe-maker, ditto
Porter John, yeoman, ditto
Starkin Robert, farmer, ditto
Sutliffe John, ditto, ditto
Vincent Robert, shoe-maker, ditto

E 2.

Wm. Coke | Wood.

Denver.

Wade William, yeoman, Denver
Wardell John, wheelwright, ditto
Wardell Abraham, ditto, ditto
White John, victualler, ditto
Wright William, farmer, Downham

Denton.

Arnesby William, farmer, Denton
Buck James, labourer, ditto
Buxton John, farmer, ditto
Button Ephraim, miller, ditto
Henley S. B. gent. ditto
Pashley William, farmer, ditto
Rayner John, farmer, Earsham
Sandby Rev. D. D. Denton
Youngs John, farmer, Wortwell

Dereham East.

Amis Thomas, confectioner, East Dereham
Adcock John, millwright, ditto
Allcock John, husbandman, ditto
Andrews John, baker, Ovington
Athill Anthony, gent. Kerdiston
Barker William, stationer, East Dereham
Barrett Robert, farmer, ditto
Bidwell Samuel, brewer, ditto
Banyard Matthew, baker, ditto
Bayfield George Clarke, farmer, ditto
Bayfield William, ditto, Welborne
Bennett George, cordwainer, Beetley
Bridges Samuel, ditto, East Dereham
Blackburne William, bricklayer, ditto
Burroughs Daniel, cordwainer, ditto
Bensly John, farmer, ditto
Baker William, ditto, Yaxham
Carr Robert, gent. East Dereham
Carr Samuel, tailor, ditto
Collison William, gent. ditto
Codd Edward, clerk, ditto
Clarke Samuel, bricklayer, ditto
Cooper Robert, butter-factor, ditto
Clements John, sen. farmer, ditto

Dereham East.

	Win.	Coke	Wod.
Clements John, farmer, Scarning			
Dukham James, patten-maker, East Dereham			
Dacke John, surgeon, ditto			
Deighton William, clerk, Whinbergh			
Eastoe John, farmer, East Dereham			
Eastoe Reuben, ditto, ditto			
Firth William, wheelwright, ditto			
Frere Edward, esq. Roydon			
Goulty Wm. linen-draper, East Dereham			
Green Samuel, schoolmaster, ditto			
Goddard Richard, grocer, ditto			
Hewitt John, M.D. Mattishall			
Hipkins Robert, farmer, East Dereham			
Heyhoe Jermyn, gent. ditto			
Howard William, jun. vintner, ditto			
Hutton Edward, clk. Barton Turf			
Ingleton Zachariah, whitesmith, ditto			
Jarvis William, tailor, East Dereham			
Kirby Henry, gent. ditto			
Knapp William, grocer, ditto			
Talman John, attorney, ditto			
Mays John, gent. Westfield			
Middleton John, gent. Whinbergh			
Mason Robert, farmer, East Dereham			
Norton Robert, miller, ditto			
Nicholson Geo. husbandman, Swanton Mor.			
Nicholson Daniel, farmer, Yaxham			
Palmer William, farmer, North Tuddenham			
Palmer Edward, husbandman, East Dereham			
Parke Thomas, labourer, Whissonset			
Pond John, builder, East Dereham			
Pond William, breeches-maker, ditto			
Philo James, cordwainer, East Dereham			
Raven Henry, gent. ditto			
Smith Wm. brazier, Burnham Westgate			
Spencer Henry, chair-maker, Hoe			
Spence Henry, chair-maker, Stanfield			
Smyth Thomas, gent. East Dereham			
Stringer James, gardener, ditto			
Taylor William, brewer, ditto			
Utten Christopher, farmer, Wendling			
Utten Robert, upholsterer, Dillington			

Dereham East.

	Win.	Coke	Wod.
Utten William, farmer, East Dereham			
Utten Robert, farmer, ditto			
Waters John, gent. Gressenhall			
Wigg Goddard, carpenter, E. Dereham			
Wigg John Goddard, grocer, ditto			
Wigg Wright, maltster, ditto	39	43	37

Dereham West.

	Win.	Coke	Wod.
Armstrong Thomas, yeoman, West Dereham			
Armstrong William, farmer, ditto			
Beckett Thomas, ditto, Stoke Ferry			
Cobb William, ditto, West Dereham			
Filbee John, carpenter, ditto			
Godfrey Marsters, farmer, ditto			
Shorten Thomas, ditto, ditto	2	3	5

Dickleburgh.

	Win.	Coke	Wod.
Abbott John, wool-comber, Dickleburgh			
Bacon John, ——, ditto			
Dix Robert, farmer, ditto			
Dye John, yeoman, ditto			
Ellis Samuel, gent. Tivetshall St. Mary			
Flowerdew Joseph, surgeon, Dickleburgh			
Gilbank Thomas, clerk, ditto			
Gissing Stephen, shopkeeper, ditto			
Goddard Thomas, farmer, ditto			
Goff William, tailor, ditto			
King William, tailor, ditto			
Lee George, gent. ditto			
Laydon Thomas, farmer, ditto			
Mickleburgh John, ditto, ditto			
Page John, ditto, ditto			
Pett Oliver, grocer, ditto			
Smith James, husbandman, ditto			
Vyse Nicholas, farmer, ditto			
Walton Samuel, ditto, ditto			
Wilton Charles, blacksmith, ditto			
Winkfield Philip, farmer, ditto	8	13	13

Didlington.

	Win.	Coke	Wod.
Spinks Wm. farmer, Wiggenhall St. Mary M.			
Wilson Robert, esq. Didlington	0	0	2

Dilham.

Frary John, yeoman, Dilham
Hannant Jeremiah, miller, ditto
Hannant Richard, farmer, ditto
Joy John, merchant, ditto
Lambert Thomas, yeoman, Ingham
Lyall John, farmer, Dilham
Mileham John, yeoman, ditto
Taylor Shepherd, farmer, ditto

Dillington.

Daniel John, farmer, Dillington
Riches Henry, ditto, ditto

Diss.

Augold John, carpenter, Diss
Barkham Thomas, cabinet-maker, ditto
Blomfield John, carpenter, ditto
Blomfield William, gent. Banham
Bird Luke, gent. Diss
Bray James, ditto, ditto
Bray Thomas, farmer, ditto
Browne Harry, esq. ditto
Brightwen George, ditto, ditto
Chittock Jeremiah, blacksmith, ditto
Corben Joseph, farmer, ditto
Curson Thomas, attorney's clerk, ditto
Dixon John, carrier, ditto
Drake Edmund, wheelwright, ditto
Dyson John, brewer, ditto
Dyson Thomas, esq. ditto
Eglinton John, tailor, ditto
Ellis William, farmer, ditto
Ellis Henry, ditto, ditto
Eaton George, manufacturer, Shelfanger
Fincham Zachariah, esq. Diss
Foulger Samuel, farmer, ditto
Farrow Thomas, carpenter, ditto
Fulcher Thomas, jun. farmer, Rushall
Fisher John, ditto, Diss
Fulcher Thomas, gent. ditto
Filby Edmund, farmer, ditto
Gobbett James, cordwainer, ditto

Win.	Coke	Wod.
6	6	2
2	2	0

Diss.

Griggs Robert, tanner, Diss
Harrison William, schoolmaster, Gissing
Howell William, cordwainer, Diss
Hubbard Robert, bricklayer, ditto
Hubbard William, husbandman, ditto
Jeffries John, farmer, ditto
Kent John, farmer, Carlton Rode
Kerry Joseph, shopkeeper, Diss
Kerry Cornelius, wheelwright, ditto
Last Timothy, ditto, ditto
Lingwood George, cabinet-maker, ditto
Manning William, clerk, ditto
Moore James, farmer, Carlton Rode
Moore Samuel, miller, Diss
Newson William, tanner, ditto
Newby John, publican, ditto
Pimm William, farmer, ditto
Poole John, worsted-weaver, ditto
Pretty Ellis, ditto, ditto
Quantrell John, linen-weaver, ditto
Rich John, cabinet-maker, ditto
Sands John, baker, ditto
Sands Thomas, miller, ditto
Scrivener John, baker, ditto
Sheriffe Robert, esq. ditto
Simpson Wm. Wooley, gent. ditto
Spurdens Richard, farmer, ditto
Spurdens Robert, linen-weaver, ditto
Stoughton Robert, esq. ditto
Sharman John, surgeon, ditto
Vyse James, currier, ditto
Walpole Robert, gent. ditto
Waller John, grocer, ditto
Whaites John, sen. gent. ditto
Womack George, linen-weaver, ditto
Wiseman Benjamin, gent. ditto
Wiseman John, ditto, ditto
Whaite Thomas, glazier, ditto
Woodward T. J. esq. ditto

Win.	Coke	Wod.
35	43	30

Ditchingham.

	Win.	Coke.	Wod.
Baker Samuel, gent. Chedgrave			
Baker John, ditto, Knapton			
Bedingfield John James, esq. Ditchingham			
Day John, farmer, ditto			
Denny Thomas, ditto, Toftmonks			
Long John, ditto, Ditchingham			
Miles John, linen-weaver, ditto			
Spence William, farmer, ditto			
Stanford William, ditto, ditto			
	5	5	5

Docking.

	Win.	Coke.	Wod.
Burgis Robert, butcher, Docking			
Curtis Philip, cordwainer, ditto			
Drake Matthew, gent. Burnham Westgate			
Dusgate Thomas, esq. Little Dunham			
Dunn William, grocer, Docking			
Frost Henry Cory, miller, ditto			
Hacon Thomas, carpenter, Rockland			
Hare Edward, clerk, Docking			
Humphrey George, miller, Bircham Magna			
Joy Thomas, surgeon, Docking			
Pitchers William, labourer, ditto			
Shaul Edm. surgeon, Wiggenhall St. M. Mag			
Silence Nicholas, gardener, Docking			
Sinkler Charles, gent. ditto			
Spurgen George, farmer, Brancaster			
	13	15	1

Downham.

	Win.	Coke.	Wod.
Baldwin William, miller, Downham			
Bird Benjamin, gent. ditto			
Balding John, mason, ditto			
Bell Isaac, victualler, ditto			
Brighton Thomas, gent. ditto			
Brighton William, victualler, ditto			
Carter Abraham, yeoman, ditto			
Coates William, gent. Tilney St. Lawrence			
Dixon Thos. Shuckforth, gent. Saham Toney			
Ellis Edward, carpenter, Downham			
Elsey Richard, glazier, ditto			
Flower Jonathan, carpenter, ditto			
Franklin Thomas, innkeeper, ditto			
Green Robert, baker, ditto			

F

Downham.

	Win.	Coke.	Wod.
Gillingham Thomas, bricklayer, Downham			
Goodchild John, ditto, ditto			
Hacon J. G. schoolmaster, ditto			
Hagon Thomas, sen. carpenter, Rockland			
Hampson James, liquor-merchant, Downham			
Harris John, tailor, ditto			
Hourston Thomas, ditto, ditto			
Lemon William, gent. ditto			
Mann John, ditto, Tilney St. Lawrence			
Martin William, ditto, Southery			
Merrington Edward, miller, Downham			
Miller William, gent. Denver			
Parke Gilbert, clerk, Downham			
Pidgeon Martin, farmer, ditto			
Rawling William, gent. ditto			
Rosher Thomas, ditto, ditto			
Rosher Thomas, jun. ditto, ditto			
Rose William, blacksmith, Upwell			
Say William, esq. Downham			
Saffery Edward, gent. ditto			
Saffery Henry, ditto, ditto			
Simpson William, farmer, Snettisham			
Smith Wm. James, Druggist, Wimbotsham			
Stevens John, draper, Downham			
Taylor John, gent. ditto			
Tiffen Roger, ditto, Wimbotsham			
Turner John, labourer, Thetford			
Turner John, farmer, ditto			
Thorogood Robert A. printer, Downham			
Thompson Edmund, farmer, ditto			
Thompson Robert, ditto, Setchy			
Tiffen William, clerk, Downham			
Wales Thomas, surgeon, ditto			
Watson James, baker, ditto			
Weston Jonas, bailiff, ditto			
Weston William, yeoman, ditto			
Wingfield Joseph, ditto, ditto			
Wright Thomas, grocer, ditto			
Wiles William, farmer, ditto			
Wyes John G. baker, ditto			
	45	45	9

Drayton.

Edwards William, farmer, Drayton
Eaton Charles, esq. ditto
Payne Edward Daws, esq. ditto

Win.	Coke	Wod.
3	3	0

Dunham Great.

Bacon John, husbandman, Great Dunham
Bament James, kiddier, ditto
Dalton Chamberlin, esq. ditto
Dalton Chamberlin, farmer, ditto
Dunger John, gardener, ditto
Dunger John, farmer, ditto
Harvey Richard, gelder, Stanfield
King Samuel, gent. Great Downham
Rix Thomas, farmer, ditto
Trundle Robert, ditto, ditto

Win.	Coke	Wod.
7	9	4

Dunham Little.

Ball Anthony, farmer, Little Dunham
Hey William, husbandman, ditto
Jackson John, farmer, ditto
Jowett Henry, clerk, ditto
Kirbell Richard, tanner, Hockwold

Win.	Coke	Wod.
1	2	4

Dunston.

Carpenter Robert, farmer, Pulham Market
Long Robert Churchman, clerk, Dunston

Win.	Coke	Wod.
0	0	2

Dunton.—Gallow Hundred.

Barber John, farmer, Frettenham

Win.	Coke	Wod.
1	1	0

Earsham.

Aggras Robert, gent. Starston
Banham James, weaver, Earsham
Banham John, higler, ditto
Butcher Mark, gent. Wortwell
Buxton Richard, farmer, Earsham
Clarke Thomas, miller, ditto
Fickling Benjamin, husbandman, Topcroft
Mildred Thomas, farmer, Saxlingham
Spilling John, ditto, Earsham
Spilling Thomas, gent. Bedingham

Win.	Coke	Wod.
10	10	0

Easton.

Badcock Thomas, blacksmith, Deopham
Balls Thomas, farmer, Easton
Muskett Joseph, esq. Bawburgh

Win.	Coke	Wod.
3	3	0

Eccles.

Ames James, yeoman, Eccles
Empson Robert, farmer, ditto
Gooch John, gent. Kenninghall

Win.	Coke	Wod.
1	1	2

Edgefield.

Bishop John, farmer, Edgefield
Ellis Henry, baker, ditto
Ellis William, yeoman, ditto
Ford Thomas, blacksmith, ditto
Francis Bransby, clerk, ditto
Gay Benning, farmer, Guestwick
Garrett John, gent. Briston
Minns James, farmer, Edgefield
Vale John, mariner, ditto
Weeds John, farmer, Briston

Win.	Coke	Wod.
3	4	7

Edinthorpe.

Adams Richard, clerk, Edinthorpe
Barcham John, farmer, ditto
Marjoram Thomas, ditto, ditto
Turner Charles, ditto, ditto

Win.	Coke	Wod.
2	3	2

Egmere.

Purdy Thomas, farmer, Great Walsingham
Sizeland Thomas, yeoman, Marham

Win.	Coke	Wod.
0	0	2

Ellingham.—Clavering Hundred.

Fisk Anthony, farmer, Ellingham
Gibbons John, bricklayer, ditto
Hall Roger, clerk, ditto
Johnson William, clerk, ditto
Laws William, horsedealer, Kirby Cane
Westgate Robert, farmer, Ellingham
Williams Thomas, ditto, ditto

Win.	Coke	Wod.
2	3	5

Ellingham Great.

Ayres William, weaver, Great Ellingham
Bales Thomas, labourer, ditto

Ellingham North.

Name	Win.	Coke	Wod.
Laverock John, gent. North Elmham			
Lacey Richard, bricklayer, ditto			
Long William, farmer, ditto			
Mason Samuel, butcher, ditto			
Milles Richard, esq. ditto			
Smith Thomas Feverell, miller, ditto			
Twigg Thomas, farmer, Gately	3	5	14

Elsing.

Name	Win.	Coke	Wod.
Betts John, farmer, Elsing			
Browne Robert, clerk, ditto			
Collins Benjamin, farmer, ditto			
Eggett Paul, butcher, Necton			
Farrow John, yeoman, Elsing			
Filby Thomas, farmer, ditto			
Kent William, shoe-maker, ditto			
Norton William, carpenter, Sparham			
Palmer Richard, miller, Elsing			
Ward Thomas, gent. North Tuddenham	1	1	9

Emneth.

Name	Win.	Coke	Wod.
Batterham Robert, farmer, Emneth			
Bird John, ditto, ditto			
Boyce John, ditto, ditto			
Bradley George, ditto, Walsoken			
Haynes John, ditto, Emneth			
Hall William, ditto, ditto			
Hill Thomas, ditto, Outwell			
Hill Joseph, ditto, Upwell			
Jewson John, ditto, Emneth			
Marshall James, ditto, ditto			
Merrell John, labourer, ditto			
Metcalf Anthony, ditto, ditto			
Neale William, farmer, ditto			
Timpenny Thomas, ditto, ditto	10	7	5

Erpingham.

Barwick Robert, farmer, Briston
Bond Robert, yeoman, Erpingham
Browne William, ditto, Colthorpe
Cooper Thomas, cordwainer, Erpingham
Cook William, yeoman, ditto

Ellingham Great.

Name	Win.	Coke	Wod.
Barnhard John, farmer, Great Ellingham			
Barnard Robert, ditto, ditto			
Brook Robert, ditto, ditto			
Burch Matthew, turner, ditto			
Daynes John, farmer, ditto			
Dennis Benjamin, victualler, ditto			
Garnham John, gent. ditto			
Hasell Reuben, farmer, ditto			
Houchen Robert, cordwainer, ditto			
How James, farmer, ditto			
Kerrison Richard, ditto, ditto			
Kiddell William, ditto, ditto			
Morphew Thomas, labourer, ditto			
Palmer Edward, farmer, East Harling			
Towler Jeffery, ditto, Great Ellingham			
Turner Benjamin, ditto, ditto			
Turner John, ditto, ditto			
Warren William, victualler, ditto			
Warren John, farmer, ditto			
Wilkin Edward, ditto, ditto			
Wiggett Thomas, ditto, ditto	3	0	23

Ellingham Little.

Name	Win.	Coke	Wod.
Bond Thomas, clerk, Little Ellingham			
Branford William, sen. farmer, ditto			
Browne John, ditto, ditto			
Browne John, ditto, ditto			
English John, ditto, Hardingham			
Leath Cook, ditto, Great Fransham			
Spurgeon John, ditto, Little Ellingham	1	1	6

Elmham North.

Bliss John, farmer, Elmham
Bradfield Charles, ditto, ditto
Bream Thomas Rudd, ditto, Beetley
Chambers William, gent. North Elmham
Debenham John, surgeon, Worthing
Fisher Money, farmer, Stanfield
Fisher Richard, ditto, North Elmham
Girling William, gent. Yaxham
Hawes John, cooper, North Elmham
Herring Thomas, clerk, ditto

Erpingham.

Name	Win.	Coke	Wod.
Cubitt John, gent. Erpingham			
Cubitt Woolmer, gent. ditto			
Cubitt Woolmer Richard, ditto, Ingworth			
Churchill Joseph, clerk, Blickling			
Hall Daniel, liquor-merchant, Erpingham			
Harmer John, bricklayer, ditto			
Hutchin Joseph, w. weaver, Briningham			
Marsh William Heath, clerk, Calthorp			
Paul William, yeoman, Gresham			
Wicks Rice, yeoman, Banningham			
Woolsey John, jun. ditto, Burgh			
	6	7	10

Fakenham.

Name	Win.	Coke	Wod.
Back John, thatcher, Hempton			
Brett William, tailor, Little Snoring			
Burrell William, barber, Great Snoring			
Crofts John, clerk, Whissonset			
Capes Theop. stone-mason, Gt. Ryburgh			
Drane William, carrier, ditto			
Edgar Thomas, surgeon, Fakenham			
Green Henry, farmer, Horningtoft			
Green William, miller, Fakenham			
Heath, John, M. D. ditto			
Howlett Robert, farmer, East Rudham			
Hubbard Thomas, tailor, South Creak			
Ivory John, draper, Caston			
Jones Daniel, esq. Alethorpe			
Norris Charles, clerk, Fakenham			
Potter Samuel, farmer, Wighton			
Readwin Henry, carpenter, Fakenham			
Readwn John, cabinet-maker, Brisley			
Skrimshire Thomas, clerk, Hockham			
Withers Roger, gent. Stibbard			
	19	19	2

Felbrigg.

Name	Win.	Coke	Wod.
Farrow John, labourer, Repps North			
Hicks John, gent. Cromer			
Lukin George William, D. D. Felbrigg			
Miles Edmund, farmer, Burlingham			
Windham the Rt. Hon. William, Felbrigg			
	5	5	0

Felthorpe.

Name	Win.	Coke	Wod.
Betts John, farmer, Felthorpe			
Miller Thomas, yeoman, ditto			
Norman Stephen, farmer, ditto			
Spurling Stephen, ditto, ditto			
Utten James, yeoman, ditto			
	3	4	1

Felmingham.

Name	Win.	Coke	Wod.
Cook John, farmer, Felmingham			
Cook Edmund, yeoman, ditto			
Cook Charles, miller, ditto			
Hayne John, farmer, ditto			
King Doods, paper-maker, ditto			
Mayes Thomas, yeoman, Skeyton			
Moore William, sen. farmer, Felmingham			
Olifant James, gent. North Walsham			
Sewell William, yeoman, Skeyton			
Wright Samuel, farmer, Wymondham			
	4	4	7

Feltwell St. Mary and Nicholas.

Name	Win.	Coke	Wod.
Banham William, farmer, Feltwell			
Banham Edward, ditto, Southery			
Drake John, blacksmith, Feltwell			
Eyres John, farmer, ditto			
Forster William, collar-maker, ditto			
Fuller John, gent. ditto			
Gaverick Phil. farmer, ditto			
Hollox John, labourer, ditto			
Howes Thomas, butcher, ditto			
Jacobs Thomas, aledraper, ditto			
Killingworth Anthony, farmer, ditto			
Killingworth Anthony, ditto, ditto			
Killingworth Robert, carrier, ditto			
Lascock John, breeches-maker, ditto			
Leonard John, labourer, ditto			
Mayes Thomas, ditto, ditto			
Pryer William, farmer, ditto			
Palmer Robert, blacksmith, ditto			
Pritchard Henry, clerk, ditto			
Parsons Robert, bricklayer, ditto			
Pearson Matthew, farmer, ditto			
Pearson Orsborn, ditto, ditto			
Pearson Edward, ditto, ditto			

Feltwell St. Mary and Nicholas.

Name	Win.	Coke	Wod.
Rudland Thomas, cordwainer, Feltwell			
Rudland John, farmer, ditto			
Rudland Benjamin, ditto, ditto			
Rolfe Joseph, labourer, ditto			
Russell Robert, baker, ditto			
Richardson John, millwright, ditto			
Richardson John, millwright, ditto			
Russell John, farmer, ditto			
Siggoc John, aledraper, ditto			
Simpson Thomas, farmer, ditto			
Spencer Porter, thatcher, ditto			
Spinks John, tailor, ditto			
Spinks Abraham, farmer, ditto			
Stallon Richard, ditto, ditto			
Stevenson Richard, clerk, ditto			
Tompson William, gent. ditto			
Tokelove Robert, wheelwright, ditto			
Tuddenham Thomas, labourer, ditto			
West Thomas, jun. farmer, ditto			
Ward Thomas, labourer, ditto			
Ward John, ditto, ditto			
Watson Richard, gardener, ditto			
Whiteman Henry, farmer, ditto			
Whiteman Edward, ditto, ditto			
Willett John, ditto, ditto			
Witmore William, cordwainer, ditto			
Young Thomas, farmer, ditto	13	16	37

Fersfield.

Name	Win.	Coke	Wod.
Algar James, farmer, Fersfield			
Breadstreet William, ditto, South Lopham			
Carter Samuel, clerk, Felthorpe			
Carleton James, farmer, Fersfield			
Clamp Thomas, ditto, ditto			
Smith Thomas, ditto, ditto	4	4	2

Filby.—East Flegg.

Name	Win.	Coke	Wod.
Ade William, labourer, Filby			
Crowe Benjamin, shoe-maker, ditto			
Dixon Robert, farmer, ditto			
Everson James, shopkeeper, ditto			
Frosdyke Edward, husbandman, ditto			

G

Filby.—East Flegg.

Name	Win.	Coke	Wod.
Green Thomas, husbandman, Filby			
Humphrey Benjamin, blacksmith, ditto			
Jay John, gardener, ditto			
Jay Robert, ditto, ditto			
Juby Thomas, farmer, ditto			
Lucas Charles, esq. ditto			
Martins Francis, gardener, Yarmouth			
Narborough William, farmer, Filby			
Narford John, ditto, ditto			
Skoyles Thomas, wheelwright, ditto			
Tennant Francis, thatcher, ditto			
Ward Edward, blacksmith, ditto	3	5	14

Fincham.—Clackclose.

Name	Win.	Coke	Wod.
Aylmer George, farmer, Fincham			
Barsham Edmund, gent. ditto			
Bland Thomas, carpenter, ditto			
Bull Joseph, farmer, ditto			
Burton Clement, glover, ditto			
Bywater John, farmer, ditto			
Camplin Thomas, ditto, ditto			
Doe William, ditto, ditto			
Fisher Matthew, yeoman, ditto			
Forby Robert, clerk, ditto			
Garman James, gardener, ditto			
Hebgin John, farmer, ditto			
Knock John, shoe-maker, ditto			
Mawby Isaac, farmer, ditto			
Parish James, grocer, Marham			
Walker Stephen, tailor, Fincham			
Watson John, shoe-maker, ditto			
Wright Thomas, blacksmith, ditto			
Young Thomas, grocer, ditto			
Young John, glazier, ditto	5	6	16

Flitcham.—Freebridge Lynn.

Name	Win.	Coke	Wod.
Billing T. wheelwright, Weasingham All St.			
Blomfield John, farmer, Billingford			
Blomfield Miles, ditto, Foulsham			
Burrell Martin, ditto, Flitcham			
England George, ditto, Hindringham	5	5	0

	Win.	Coke	Wod.

Flordon.
Livock Henry, farmer, Tasburgh

Fordham.
Canham Anthony S. gent. Fordham
Creasy John, ditto, Hilgay
Goldsmith John, yeoman, Gimmingham
Wright John, farmer, Northwold

(0 · 0 · 1)

Forncet St. Mary.
Aggs Thomas, farmer, Mattishall
Doe James, gent. Forncet St. Mary
Spicer John, farmer, ditto

(4 · 4 · 0)

Forncet St. Peter.
Blomfield William, miller, Forncet St. Peter
Brock Leonard, husbandman, ditto
Browne James, gent. ditto
Carver Charles, clerk, Topcroft
Colman Jeremiah, farmer, Tacolneston
Doe James, ditto, Forncet St. Peter
Hardy Isaac, ditto, ditto
Jeck Thomas, clerk, Rectory of Forncet
Park Thomas, gent. Forncet St. Peter
Sewell Robert, labourer, ditto
Spink James, bricklayer, ditto
Stackard Thomas, farmer, ditto
Websdale Charles, ditto, ditto

(1 · 2 · 2)

Foulden.
Codling Edward, cordwainer, Foulden
Dodds Peter, farmer, ditto
Fendick Francis, husbandman, ditto
Goat John, cordwainer, ditto
Horrex Anthony, gent. ditto
Horrex Edmund, ditto, Gooderstone
Kiddell William, husbandman, Foulden
Reynolds Thomas, carpenter, ditto
Reynolds John, farmer, ditto
Reynolds Robert, gent. ditto
Richardson John, farmer, ditto
Roberts John, ditto, ditto
Scales John, aledraper, ditto

(11 · 12 · 2)

G 2

	Win.	Coke	Wod.

Foulden.
Syzehall George, gent. Foulden
Wells Thomas, cordwainer, ditto

Foulsham.
Archer James, grocer, Foulsham
Blanchflower John, innkeeper, ditto
Fidgett James, currier, ditto
Girling John Andrews, farmer, ditto
Hunt James, grocer, Reepham
Mayes John, gent. Foulsham
Munton John, grocer, ditto
Norris George, clerk, Guist
Pike John, gent. Foxley
Quarles Thomas Francis, ditto, Foulsham
Young John, farmer, Walsoken

(6 · 8 · 9)

Foxley.
Middleton John, farmer, Bawdeswell
Neal William, dealer, Foxley

(7 · 6 · 5)

Framlingham Pigot.
Browne Robert, tailor, Framlingham Pigot
Howes William, esq. ditto
Thurston Robert, farmer, ditto
Youngs Robert, farmer, ditto

(2 · 2 · 0)

Framlingham Earl.
Blancks John, clerk, Framlingham Earl
Rigby Edward, esq. ditto

(3 · 3 · 1)

Fransham Little.
Buscall Matthew, gent. Little Fransham
Pooley Peter, farmer, ditto
Spilling Samuel, gardener, Mattishall
Swatman Edward, clerk, Little Fransham
Watling William, farmer, ditto

(2 · 2 · 0)

Freethorpe.
Chapman John, butcher, Freethorpe
Groom Edward, farmer, ditto
Jary Edward ditto, Wickhampton

(0 · 1 · 5)

Freethorpe.

	Win.	Coke	Wod.
Jenkinson George, blacksmith, Freethorpe			
Read Trivitt, farmer, Halvergate	4	4	1

Frenze.

	Win.	Coke	Wod.
Smith Hammont, farmer, Frenze	0	1	1

Frettenham.

	Win.	Coke	Wod.
Carthus Mordaunt, clerk, Frettenham			
Drake Thomas, farmer, Scarning			
Gedge William, ditto, Horstead			
Prinfall William, aledraper, Frettenham			
Read Thomas, farmer, Salhouse	1	1	4

Fransham Great.

	Win.	Coke	Wod.
Beare Robert, farmer, Great Fransham			
Bensly Henry, ditto, ditto			
Buck John, clerk, ditto			
Case Thomas Henry, farmer, ditto			
Drosier John, ditto, ditto			
Mann Richard, publican, ditto			
Rallison Thomas, farmer, ditto			
Wellingham Edward, ditto, ditto	4	5	4

Fritton.

	Win.	Coke	Wod.
Feltham James, cordwainer, Hardwick			
Fulcher James, farmer, Fritton			
Glasspoole Henry, ditto, Yarmouth			
Jermyn Benjamin, ditto, Fritton			
Pettingall John, ditto, Denton			
Websdell William, ditto, Fritton	5	5	1

Fundenhall.

	Win.	Coke	Wod.
Borking James, farmer, Fundenhall			
Harvey Robert, farmer, ditto			
Harvey James, ditto, ditto			
Howard John, gent. ditto			
Howard John, clerk, Morley St. Botolph			
Newman Daniel, farmer, Little Brand			
Turner Jon. carpenter, Forncett St. Peter			
Waller Fuller, farmer, Ashwelthorpe			
Youngman Edward, ditto, Fundenhall	2	2	7

Fulmodeston.

	Win.	Coke	Wod.
Browne Repps, clerk, Fulmodeston			
Greengrass William, pump-maker, ditto			
Nurse Edmund, miller, Croxton			
Rayner Thomas, farmer, Fulmodeston			
Rix Charles, ditto, ditto			
Sandiford Peter, clerk, ditto	6	4	1

Garboldisham.

	Win.	Coke	Wod.
Baker John, farmer, Garboldisham			
Bulton John, miller, Diss			
Cauldwell John, farmer, Garboldisham			
Chittock Benjamin, ditto, ditto			
Cooke John, ditto, ditto			
Cooke William, ditto, South Lopham			
Carly Thomas, ditto, Garboldisham			
Crooke John, tailor, ditto			
Germany Thomas, farmer, ditto			
Kemp William, husbandman, ditto			
Linstead Henry, sadler, ditto			
Molineux Charles S. clerk, ditto			
Peck Richard, farmer, ditto			
Stubbings James, ditto, ditto			
Tillett Leonard, carpenter, ditto			
Tillett John, ditto, ditto			
Worby Robert, husbandman, ditto	5	11	12

Garvestone.

	Win.	Coke	Wod.
Barnes John, farmer, Garvestone			
Bidwell Richard, husbandman, E. Dereham			
Palmer Thomas, gent. Thuxton			
Payne John, husbandman, Garvestone			
Rayner John, farmer, ditto			
Staines Edward, ditto, ditto			
Stringer William, ditto, ditto	3	5	4

Gately.

	Win.	Coke	Wod.
Doy Charles, chimney-sweeper, Gately			
Griggs Money, farmer, ditto			
Howell James, farmer, Beeston	0	0	3

Gatesend.

	Win.	Coke	Wod.
Hall William, farmer, Hindringham	0	1	1

Gaywood.

Etches John, tanner, Gaywood
Gunns John, carpenter, King's Lynn
Holden Joseph, farmer, Gaywood
Long William, baker, King's Lynn
Plowright William, miller, ditto
Powell Robert, farmer, ditto
Smith Edgeley, publican, ditto
Walker Stephen, miller, Wiggenhall St. Ger.

Win.	Coke	Wod.
5	6	3

Gayton.

Kendle William, blacksmith, Grimstone
Large Luke, farmer, Gayton
Marsters Thomas, gent. King's Lynn
Robinson Robert, bricklayer, Gayton
Smith Thomas, miller, ditto
Trundle William, farmer, West Bradenham

Win.	Coke	Wod.
4	3	2

Geldestone.

Boon Richard, farmer, Geldestone
Bristow Isaac, ditto, Aldeby
Dowson B. U. merchant, Geldestone
Kerrich Thomas, esq. ditto
Spilling James, gent. ditto

Win.	Coke	Wod.
3	3	2

Gillingham All Saints.

Alexander R. wheelwright, Gillingham St. M.
Bury John, bricklayer, Gillingham
Chapman Thomas, farmer, Geldestone
Lewis John, clerk, Gillingham
Marsh William, farmer, ditto
Shaw Samuel, builder, ditto
Wright Richard, carpenter, Kirby Cane

Win.	Coke	Wod.
2	2	5

Gillingham St. Mary.

Thacker John, cordwainer, Gillingham St. M.

Win.	Coke	Wod.
0	0	1

Gimmingham.

Bayfield William, yeoman, Gimmingham
Crane William, ditto, ditto
Cremer John, esq. ditto
Gardner Philip, D. D. ditto
Gunton John, gent. ditto

Gimmingham.

Hall Thomas, carpenter, Gimmingham
Mexfield Robert, yeoman, ditto
Mileham John, carpenter, ditto
Press Thomas, yeoman, Southrepps
Thompson James, ditto, Gimmingham

Win.	Coke	Wod.
3	2	8

Gissing.

Bailey John, farmer, Garboldisham
Bolton George, ditto, Gissing
Carleton William, ditto, ditto
Gilbert John, gent. ditto
Howman Edward, clerk, ditto
Mickleburgh Samuel, farmer, Shelfanger
Spurdens William, ditto, Gissing
Womack William B. miller, ditto

Win.	Coke	Wod.
6	7	2

Glanford.

Leman John, yeoman, Gresham

Win.	Coke	Wod.
1	1	0

Godwick.

Bell John Brandford, farmer, Oxwick
Hoste Dixon, clerk, Tittleshall

Win.	Coke	Wod.
2	2	0

Gooderstone.

Brooks James, farmer, Gooderstone
Garrad Samuel, ditto, ditto
Lambert Francis, ditto, ditto
Palmer Thomas, ditto, ditto

Gresham.

Arden Edward, clerk, Gresham
Black John, yeoman, ditto
Clarke James, ditto, ditto
Critoph Robert, miller, ditto
Field John, carpenter, ditto
Fuller Richard, lime-burner, ditto
Lorke Samuel, farmer, Hickling
Mayes Robert, yeoman, Baconsthorpe
Raunce Jonathan, ditto, Gresham
Scott John, ditto, ditto
Shore James, ditto, Aylmerton
Shore James, ditto, Gresham

Win.	Coke	Wod.
1	1	3
12	12	0

Gressenhall.

Name	Win.	Coke	Wod.
Bond John, farmer, Gressenhall			
Blomfield Brown, publican, ditto			
Butcher Robert, blacksmith, Shipdham			
Clements John, cordwainer, Gressenhall			
Coleman Ambrose, butcher, ditto			
Coleman Jeremiah, farmer, ditto			
Dade William, gent. East Dereham			
Hewitt John, farmer, Gressenhall			
Lynn James, husbandman, ditto			
Nicholls Moses, linen-weaver, ditto			
Payne James, gardener, ditto			
Rawling Samuel, farmer, ditto			
Rother John, ditto, ditto			
Webb John, husbandman, ditto			
Wilkins Robert, farmer, ditto			
Winter Ambrose, ditto, Brisley	5	7	11

Grimstone.

Name	Win.	Coke	Wod.
Bissell John, farmer, Grimstone			
Brett John, clerk, ditto			
Clare John, yeoman, ditto			
Collison William, farmer, ditto			
Daville John, gent. Tilney St. Lawrence			
Howard John, farmer, Grimstone			
Hudson John, ditto, ditto			
Kenny John, malster, ditto			
Lofty John, yeoman, ditto			
Panks Robert, ditto, Roydon			
Smith Robert, carpenter, Grimstone			
Wakefield Thomas, gardener, King's Lynn	9	10	3

Giston.

Name	Win.	Coke	Wod.
Osborn William, Caston			
Smith Robert, gent. ditto	2	1	0

Guestwick.

Name	Win.	Coke	Wod.
Beals Thomas, gent. Guestwick	1	1	0

Guest.

Name	Win.	Coke	Wod.
Chaplin Thomas, liquor-merchant, Guest			
Colls Thomas, yeoman, ditto			
Dewing Edward, gent. ditto			

Guest.

Name	Win.	Coke	Wod.
Doomer Robert, farmer, Guest			
Goddard John, ditto, Briston			
Robertson William, yeoman, Guest			
Russell James, farmer, ditto	0	0	7

Gunton.

Name	Win.	Coke	Wod.
Fowler Thomas, esq. Yarmouth	1	1	0

Gunthorpe.

Name	Win.	Coke	Wod.
Barwick John, farmer, Brinton			
Bunn Thomas, gardener, Gunthorpe			
Colyer Charles, clerk, ditto			
England Thos. Waller, yeoman, ditto			
Fitt Robert, gardener, ditto			
Hunn Clement, carpenter, ditto			
Pleasance David, farmer, ditto			
Read Edward, yeoman, ditto			
Sprunt Matthew, ditto, ditto	8	8	1

Hackford.—Forehoe.

Name	Win.	Coke	Wod.
Bush John, husbandman, Hackford			
Duffell William, farmer, ditto			
Granger John, ditto, ditto			
Kerrison Noah, ditto, ditto			
Taylor Thomas, ditto, ditto			
Thorne Robert, ditto, ditto			
Wade John, ditto, ditto			

Hackford---Eynsford.

Name	Win.	Coke	Wod.
Austin John, butcher, Reepham			
Austin Thomas, ditto, Hackford			
Bircham Samuel, gent. Whitwell			
Burton Joseph, butcher, Hackford			
Burcham William, gent. ditto			
Burcham Robert, farmer, ditto			
Dunham Michael, carpenter, ditto			
Grand Richard, blacksmith, ditto			
Howke Robert, farmer, Reepham			
Leeds Stephen, cordwainer, Hackford			
More J. B, grocer, ditto			
Scurl Robert, baker, ditto			
Sewell Samuel, carpenter, ditto	2	2	5

Hackford.—Eynsford.

	Win.	Coke	Wod.
Symonds William, schoolmaster, Hackford			
Williams David, surgeon, ditto	12	12	3

Hadiscoe.

	Win.	Coke	Wod.
Browne Robert, husbandman, Hadiscoe			
Burroughes Owen, ditto, ditto			
Dann Ambrose, labourer, ditto			
Dawson Richard, gent. ditto			
Ellison Thomas, clerk, ditto			
Elliot Jacob, gent. ditto			
Forder Joseph, bricklayer, ditto			
Ginnis William, labourer, ditto			
Grimmer George, farmer, ditto			
Grimmer John, ditto, ditto			
Grimmer Samuel, ditto, ditto			
Johnson James, labourer, ditto			
Key John, shopkeeper, Yarmouth			
Mace Jacob, farmer, Hadiscoe			
Rivett John, ditto, ditto			
Walpole Robert, gardener, ditto			
Wales John, farmer, ditto			
Wright Edmund, husbandman, ditto	3	5	15

Hales.

	Win.	Coke	Wod.
Buck Robert, farmer, Toft Monks			
Freston Anthony, sen. farmer, Hales			
Haze John, ditto, ditto			
Mickleburgh John, ditto, ditto			
Nichols William, ditto, Toft Monks	3	2	2

Halvergate.

	Win.	Coke	Wod.
Atkinson Anthony, bricklayer, Halvergate			
Bately Robert, farmer, ditto			
Davy John, ditto, ditto			
Gillett John, ditto, ditto			
Gillett William, ditto, ditto			
Shepherd John, vintner, Acle			
Wyand Benjamin, school-master, Halvergate	5	5	3

Hanworth.

Bacon John, husbandman, Wood-dalling
Chapman George, yeoman, Thwaite

H 2

Hanworth.

	Win.	Coke	Wod.
Doughty Robert Lee, esq. Hanworth			
Hepworth John, clerk, ditto	3	3	1

Happisburgh.

	Win.	Coke	Wod.
Armstrong John, farmer, Happisburgh			
Bates Robert, shopkeeper, ditto			
Betts Philip, wheelwright, ditto			
Carr Thomas, farmer, ditto			
Cater Thomas, yeoman, ditto			
Gaze John, farmer, ditto			
Harvey John, miller, ditto			
Howes William, farmer, ditto			
Ingall Samuel, gardener, ditto			
Olley John, farmer, ditto			
Pilgrim James, ditto, ditto			
Postle John, carpenter, ditto			
Saul John, farmer, ditto			
Sisley Alexander, ditto, ditto			
Summers Robert, ditto, ditto			
Shepherd John, ditto, ditto			
Webster Rice, yeoman, ditto			
Youngs William, farmer, ditto	3	2	18

Hapton.

	Win.	Coke	Wod.
Fannell James, carpenter, Hapton			
Hart Charles, farmer, Tasburgh			
Hart John, ditto, Hapton			
Parslee Robert, miller, ditto			
Tremlet John, clerk, ditto	4	5	0

Hardingham.

	Win.	Coke	Wod.
Alpe Hamond, esq. Hardingham			
Belson Bays, wheelwright, ditto			
Brook John, farmer, ditto			
Doe William, ditto, ditto			
Harwin William, blacksmith, ditto			
Haythorpe James, carpenter, Hingham			
Juby Robert, farmer, Hardingham			
Neave Charles, ditto, ditto			
Parke Francis, gent. ditto			
Rose Thomas, farmer, ditto			

Hardingham.

	Win.	Coke	Wod.
Thurling Benj. blacksmith, Hardingham			
Whiter Walter, clerk, ditto			

Hardley.

	Win.	Coke	Wod.
Duffin Joseph, farmer, Hardley	2	2	10
Gilbert Robert, ditto, Cantley			
Goddard Samuel, ditto, Hardley			

Hardwick.

	Win.	Coke	Wod.
Booty Jonathan, farmer, Dickleburgh	2	2	1
Branch James, ditto, Starston			
Copping Edward, ditto, Hardwick			
George William, gent. Tivetshall			
Lighton Robert, farmer, Hardwick			
Page John, ditto, ditto			
Scales David, carpenter, ditto			
Vipond John, ditto, ditto			
Westgate David, farmer, ditto			
Wilby Richard, blacksmith, ditto	2	3	8

Hargham.

	Win.	Coke	Wod.
Bowles Matthew, farmer, Forncet St. Peter			
Leverington William, weaver, Attleburgh			

Harleston.

	Win.	Coke	Wod.
Aldous James, merchant, Harleston			
Allured John, tailor, ditto			
Carthew George, gent. ditto			
Copping Samuel, ditto, Mundham			
Doughty John, gent. Redenhall			
Gaze James, farmer, Halesworth			
Parslee Thomas, gent. ditto			
Rodwell Charles, butcher, ditto			
Scarlet Thomas, wheelwright, ditto			
Tilney Henry, schoolmaster, ditto			
Tyrrell Robert, innkeeper, Mundham	0	0	2
Wagstaffe Thomas, gent. Harleston			

Harling East.

	Win.	Coke	Wod.
Allen William, carpenter, East Harling			
Bird John Thirsby, clerk, Rockland St. Peter			
Bunnett Robert, gent. East Harling	6	9	5

Harling East.

	Win.	Coke	Wod.
Crack Henry, farmer, East Harling			
Cullum Robert, labourer, ditto			
Deane George, clerk, ditto			
Everett Thomas, shopkeeper, ditto			
Gorred Thomas, farmer, ditto			
Garrett Benjamin, yeoman, ditto			
Herold John, thatcher, ditto			
Knight Robert, farmer, ditto			
Kerrison George, ditto, ditto			
Linstead John, ditto, ditto			
Palmer William, ditto, ditto			
Peak Thomas, blacksmith, ditto			
Rodwell Henry, farmer, ditto			
Seaman Clear, labourer, ditto			
Sparrow Spicer, gent. ditto			
Tillett Thomas, farmer, ditto			
Wretham John, ditto, ditto	7	6	15

Harling West.

	Win.	Coke	Wod.
Deane Richard, clerk, West Harling			
Franks Jacob, esq. ditto	0	0	2

Harpley.

	Win.	Coke	Wod.
Buck Thomas, yeoman, Harpley			
Gotterson Samuel, yeoman, Skeyton			
Raven Nicholas J. gent. Harpley	1	2	2

Hasingham.

	Win.	Coke	Wod.
Brown Alexander, farmer, Hasingham			
Curtis John, ditto, Yarmouth			

Hautboys Great.

	Win.	Coke	Wod.
Drake Daniel, farmer, Frettenham	2	2	0

Hautboys Little.

	Win.	Coke	Wod.
Davy William, clerk, Tibenham	1	0	1

Hainford.

	Win.	Coke	Wod.
Nash James, farmer, Hainford			
Smith James, ditto, ditto	0	0	1
Worth William, esq. ditto	1	1	2

	Win.	Coke	Wod.

Heacham.
Bradfield Thomas, farmer, Heacham
Clowes Francis, ditto, Halvergate
Davey John, gent. Heacham
Eldridge John, farmer, ditto
Johnson Robert, ditto, Terrington St. Clem.
Minns Robert, carpenter, Hunstanton
Priestley Thomas, clerk, Heacham
Rolfe Edmund, esq. ditto
Slapp Henry, gent. Grimstone
Styleman Nicholas, esq. Hunstanton

9 | 9 | 1

Heckingham.
Adams Joseph, gent. Hardley
Browne William, farmer, Seething

0 | 0 | 2

Hedenham.
Bloy James, farmer, Stratton St. Mary
Feltham Thomas, ditto, Burston
Gooch Henry, ditto, Bedingham
Hannont Thomas, butcher, Hedenham
Smith Robert, farmer, ditto

1 | 1 | 4

Helhoughton.
Case Thomas, farmer, Helhoughton
Doyle John, carpenter, Hempton
Martin James, labourer, Helhoughton
Newell Thomas, farmer, ditto
Wicks George, baker, ditto

2 | 2 | 3

Hellington.
Newman Robert, farmer, Surlingham

1 | 1 | 0

Hemsby.
Bensly William, farmer, Hemsby
Church Edward, bricklayer, ditto
Copeman Robert, farmer, Stokesby
Ditcham William, bricklayer, E. Somerton
Ferrier Robert, farmer, Hemsby
Fabb Richard, ditto, ditto
Gibbs Thomas, shoe-maker, ditto
Harbord John, carpenter, ditto
Harbord Thomas, farmer, ditto

	Win.	Coke	Wod.

Hemsby.
Howard Benjamin, farmer, Hemsby
Holmes Thomas, gent. Yarmouth
Money John, wheelwright, Hemsby
Townshend Edward, schoolmaster, ditto
Waters Robert, farmer, Potter Heigham

6 | 4 | 11

Hemblington.
Benstead Wm. wheelwright, Hemblington
Gowing Richard, husbandman, Ellingham
Heath William, gent. Hemblington
Wymer John, labourer, ditto

4 | 4 | 0

Hempnall.
Adcock James, barber, Hempnall
Beckett Robert, farmer, ditto
Cockerill William, publican, ditto
Doyley Henry, farmer, ditto
Flint John, labourer, ditto
Goose William, farmer, ditto
Jenner James, ditto, Fritton
King William, ——— Hempnall
Morrison James, watch-maker, Tunstead
Nash John, publican, Hempnall
Read Jonathan, carpenter, ditto
Richards James, linen-weaver, ditto
Roberts Thomas, ——— ditto
Sporle John, labourer, ditto
Sporle Richard, farmer, ditto
Sporle Robert, weaver, ditto
Stone William, linen-weaver, ditto
Thurkettle John, farmer, ditto
Trower Robert, ditto, ditto
Wyard Wm. ditto, Rockland St. Andrew

0 | 0 | 20

Hemstead.
Smith William, farmer, Burgh St. Peter

0 | 0 | 1

Hempton.
Diggins Henry, publican, Hempton

1 | 1 | 0

Hemstead with Eccles.

	Win.	Coke	Wod.
Amis John, farmer, Hemstead			
Hewitt John, clerk, Walcot			
Littlewood John, farmer, Hemstead			
Silcock William, ditto, Hemstead	1	2	3

Herringby.

	Win.	Coke	Wod.
Denew William, farmer, Herringby			
Waters Azariah, ditto, ditto	0	0	2

Hethel.

	Win.	Coke	Wod.
Beevor Sir Thomas, bart. Hethel			
Sendall John, farmer, Redenhall	0	2	2

Hetherset.

	Win.	Coke	Wod.
Bailey John, thatcher, Hetherset			
Buckle John, esq. ditto			
Buckle Thomas Starling, ditto, ditto			
Davey William, farmer, ditto			
Edwards Bartholomew, clerk, ditto			
Hardy James, gent. ditto			
Iselin John Luke, esq. ditto			
Marsham Robert, esq. Worstead			
Norgate Thomas Starling, esq. Hetherset			
Parker John, husbandman, ditto			
Parke John, farmer, Lyng			
Smith John, ditto, Surlingham			
Wiffin John, ditto, Wymondham			1

Hevingham.

	Win.	Coke	Wod.
Alderson Joseph, clerk, Hevingham			
Curtis James, yeoman, ditto			
Rackham Thomas, ditto, ditto			
Spinks John, yeoman, ditto			
Waller James, labourer, ditto	6	9	6

Heveringland.

	Win.	Coke	Wod.
Bailey William, carpenter, King's Lynn	2	3	3
Fellowes W. H. esq. Heveringland			
West Christopher, farmer, Thornage	0	0	3

Heydon.

	Win.	Coke	Wod.
Bulwer William Earle, esq. Heydon			
Bulwer Augustine, clerk, Sall			
Chaplin Moon, grocer, Guiest			
Stokes John, labourer, Wood-dalling	3	3	1

Hickling.

	Win.	Coke	Wod.
Betts Thomas, farmer, Norton Subcorse			
Bishop Benjamin, ditto, Hickling			
Buston John, ditto, ditto			
Crowe John, ditto, Catfield			
Durrant Thomas, ditto, Hickling			
Datchman John, ditto, ditto			
Gambling John, ditto, ditto			
Gaze John, ditto. ditto			
Gedge Matthew, yeoman, ditto			
Gibbs John, farmer, ditto			
Goose Thomas, ditto, ditto			
Gravener Adam, ditto, ditto			
Kerrison George, ditto, ditto			
Newman John, ditto, ditto			
Smith William Press, clerk, Waxham			
Spauls Edward, yeoman, Hickling			
Thain John, smith, ditto			
Wright William, farmer, ditto			

Hilborough.

	Win.	Coke	Wod.
Caldwell Ralph, esq. Hilborough			
Chandler Francis, farmer, ditto			
Mower Henry, ditto, ditto			
Snelling Thomas, parish-clerk, ditto			
Youngman Norris, farmer, Saham Toney	15	16	2

Hilgay.

	Win.	Coke	Wod.
Ashley Cooper, farmer, Hilgay			
Ambrose William, farrier, ditto			
Bodger Robert, farmer, ditto			
Case Robert, ditto, ditto			
Collins Simon, ditto, ditto			
Day John, ditto, ditto			
Baum William, yeoman, ditto			
Bearsley George, bricklayer, ditto			
English Robert, yeoman, ditto	0	1	5

Hilgay.

	Win	Coke	Wod.
Fretwell William, carpenter, Denver			
Houschold William, yeoman, Hilgay			
Howse Ambrose, labourer, Methwold			
Low Thomas, farmer, Hilgay			
Ogden Thomas, millwright, ditto			
Parsley Osbert, farmer, ditto			
Porter Thomas, ditto, ditto			
Porter Thomas, jun. ditto, ditto			
Royle John, clerk, ditto			
Robinson John, farmer, ditto			
Sampson John, ditto, ditto			
Simpson Thomas, victualler, ditto			
Tompson Mathias, farmer, ditto			
Verguson Robert, yeoman, ditto			
Whitmore William, millwright, ditto			
	21	23	3

Hillington.

	Win	Coke	Wod.
Bayfield John, gent. West Winch			
Bailey John, farmer, Stanfield			
Folkes Sir Martin Browne, bart. Docking			
Norman Samuel, yeoman, Congham			
	4	4	0

Hindolvestone.

	Win	Coke	Wod.
Akers R. R. gent. Hindolvestone			
Buck George, carpenter, ditto			
Cole Baker, farmer, ditto			
Dent William, tailor, ditto			
Flack Samuel, farmer, Yarmouth			
Fox John, ditto, Hindolvestone			
Gardiner John, ditto, ditto			
King John, labourer, Hindringham			
Rising William, farmer, Filby			
Reynolds William, ditto, Hindolvestone			
Smith William, worstead-weaver, Whitwell			
Wells John, blacksmith, Hindolvestone			
White James, yeoman, ditto			
	13	13	0

Hindringham.

	Win	Coke	Wod.
Barker Charles, labourer, Hindringham			
Bayley John, thatcher, ditto			
Brett Nathaniel, carpenter, ditto			
Dent Robert, farmer, ditto			

Hindringham.

	Win.	Coke	Wod.
Graver Thomas, carpenter, Hindringham			
Lee William, farmer, ditto			
Long William, blacksmith, ditto			
Orris John, farmer, ditto			
Sands William, ditto, ditto			
Smith Robert, ditto, ditto			
Starling Robert, ditto, ditto			
Sterling William, ditto, ditto			
Thompson William, carrier, ditto			
Waters George, farmer, ditto			
Walker William, gent. Thursford			
	8	12	7

Hingham.

	Win.	Coke	Wod.
Ayton Charles, carpenter, Hingham			
Basham William, blacksmith, ditto			
Bayes John, shoe-maker, ditto			
Bayes John, horse-dealer, ditto			
Bringloe Porter, surgeon, ditto			
Bringloe Charles, gent. ditto			
Browne John Henry, clerk, ditto			
Browne John, tailor, ditto			
Buck John, shopkeeper, ditto			
Carr Thomas, innkeeper, ditto			
Chaplin Charles, labourer, Little Ellingham			
Decks Charles, gardener, Hingham			
Driver Thomas, sadler, ditto			
Dummerley Thomas, clerk, Crownthorpe			
Eke John, labourer, Weeting			
Eldred Henry, farmer, Morley St. Botolph			
Elsey George, breeches-maker, Hingham			
Elsey William, bricklayer, ditto			
Francis John, husbandman, ditto			
Gapp Isaac, ditto, ditto			
Gapp Edmund, farmer, ditto			
Gapp John, ditto, ditto			
Gapp Christopher, ditto, ditto			
Gilbert John, tailor, ditto			
Gilman S. H. L. N. attorney, ditto			
Gilman Edward Case, farmer, ditto			
Gitman Samuel, brewer, ditto			
Grave Richard, cordwainer, ditto			
Howlett Joseph, farmer, ditto			

	Win.	Coke	Wod.
Hingham.			
Hurnard William, farmer, Bradiston			—
Hurnard Robert, ditto, Hingham			—
Howard Francis, draper, ditto		—	—
Jickling George, cabinet-maker, ditto			—
Lane Israel, farmer, ditto			—
Lane Joseph, clerk, ditto			—
Lane Aaron, farmer, ditto			—
Levick Edmund, cooper, ditto			—
Lincoln John, farmer, ditto			—
Lane John, ditto, ditto			—
Matthews Richard Buck, clerk, ditto			—
Money Samuel, husbandman, ditto			—
Neve John, watch-maker, ditto			—
Pollington Thomas, wheelwright, ditto			—
Riches John, farmer, ditto			—
Roberts John, glazier, ditto			—
Semmence Robert, publican, ditto			—
Semmence James, gent. ditto			—
Semmence James, carpenter, ditto			—
Spurgeon William, farmer, ditto			—
Thorne Samuel, gent. ditto			—
Wodehouse Phil. clerk, ditto			—
Woodcock Mark, gent. ditto	—	—	
Woodrow John, ditto, ditto			—
	1	2	52
Hockering.			
Gould Thomas, farmer, Hockering		—	—
Howman Roger Freston, clerk, ditto		—	—
Howard John, farmer, ditto			—
Locket James, ditto, ditto			—
Platt Samuel, jobber, ditto	—	—	
Rackham Matthew, farmer, Brandiston	—		—
Rivett Thomas, ditto, Hockering			—
Watkin Jacob, carpenter, ditto			—
	2	3	7
Hockham.			
Calver James, carpenter, Rockland St. Peter	—	—	
Faux David, cordwainer, ditto			—
Rudling Daniel, carpenter, East Harling			—
	1	1	2
Hockwold cum Wilton.			
Allison Thomas, thatcher, Hockwold	—	—	
Baldwin Thomas, gardener, ditto	—	—	

	Win.	Coke	Wod.
Hockwold cum Wilton.			
Barnard Samuel, farmer, Hockwold	—	—	
Billingsby Edward, esq. ditto			—
Bradford William, gardener, ditto	—	—	
Burroughes Jeremiah, blacksmith, ditto	—	—	
Cock Joseph, farmer, ditto		—	
Clarke Richard, tailor, ditto			—
Eastgate Thomas, husbandman, Feltwell	—	—	
Field William, blacksmith, Hockwold			—
Gore John, farmer, ditto			—
Grimmer Robert, ditto, Wilton	—		—
King William, ditto, Hockwold			—
Lamb William, bricklayer, ditto			—
Lambert William, carpenter, Feltwell	—	—	
Lambert Daniel, ditto, Hockwold	—	—	
Morley John, Bricklayer, ditto	—	—	
Morley John, cordwainer, ditto	—	—	
Newton Thomas, farmer, ditto	—	—	
Norman Francis, ditto, ditto			—
Pearson Henry, gardener, ditto			—
Poole Simon, gent. ditto	—	—	
Spinks Abraham, farmer, Feltwell			—
Thickpenny John, ditto, Hockwold			—
Tilney Henry, clerk, ditto			—
	13	13	12
Hoe.			
Bowles Clare, farmer, Mattishall	—	—	
Grounds Thomas, ditto, Swanton Morley	—	—	
Munnings Thomas Crowe, clerk, Hoe		—	—
Sterling William, horse-dealer, Thursford	—	—	
Ward Isaac, farmer, Hoe	—	—	
Wright Thomas, ditto, East Dereham	—	—	
	5	6	1
Hockham.			
Dover James, esq. Great Hockham		—	
Leist William, farmer, Ranworth			—
	0	1	1
Holme Runcton.			
Adlington Robert, farmer, Watlington	—	—	
Bell Henry, jun. clerk, Terrington St. John	—	—	
Gutheridge Thomas, farmer, Runcton Holme			—
Minnick Charles, yeoman, ditto	—	—	
	3	3	1

Holt.
Wigg John Wright, bricklayer, Holt
Withers William, attorney, ditto
Wildie William, blacksmith, Beetley

Holveston.
Woolsey Robert, farmer, Alpington

Honing.
Cole John, farmer, Honing
Cubitt Thomas, esq. ditto
Gage Benjamin, farmer, ditto
Haines George, ditto, ditto
Howard John, smith, ditto
Mason William, yeoman, Cromer

Honingham.
Beevor Arthur, esq. Honingham
Ringer John, miller, ditto
Tubby William, carpenter, Bawburgh

Horning.
Bacon Joshua, yeoman, Mundesley
Barwick Anthony, clerk, Acle
Grimes Charles, gent. Horning
Jay John, farmer, ditto
Juniper Henry, yeoman, ditto
Lea Joseph, malster, ditto

Horningtoft.
Brandford Benjamin, farmer, Horningtoft
Franklin John, ditto, ditto
Franklin John, ditto, ditto

Horsey.
Nichols J. husbandman, West Somerton
Rising Robert, gent. Horsey

Horsford.
Andrews Robert, innkeeper, Cawston
Bunn John, farmer, Horsham St. Faiths'
Day John, clerk, Horsford

Win.	Coke	Wod.
18	19	5
0	0	1
0	0	6
3	1	2
2	4	4
2	2	0
0	0	2

Holme Hale.
Copsie James, cordwainer, Holme Hale
Gainsbury Daniel, carpenter, ditto
Gibson William, farmer, ditto
Lacey William, farmer, ditto
Lock John, ditto, ditto
Palfrey Richard, miller, ditto
Percival Thomas, shopkeeper, ditto
Powley Samuel, thatcher, ditto
Stratton Thomas farmer, ditto
Weston William, ditto, ditto
Whitby James, ditto, ditto
Younge Thomas, clerk, ditto

Holme, next the Sea.
Holley John, esq. Holme next the Sea
Mayes John, yeoman, ditto
Nelson Matthew, farmer, ditto
Richardson Richard, ditto, Brancaster
Stannard John, ditto, Tilney St. Laurence

Holt.
Athow Thomas, cooper, Holt
Carr John, shoe-maker, Holt
Cheatle Robert, hat-maker, ditto
Cranefield James, wheelwright, ditto
Drozier Thomas, gent. Hunworth
Keymer Robert, farmer, Salthouse
King John, ditto Holt
King Robert, sen. gent. ditto
Leak J. C. clerk, ditto
Lynes Joseph, blacksmith, ditto
Matsell William, yeoman, ditto
Middleton John, basket-maker, Hunworth
Moore James, attorney, Forncet St. Peter
Massingham Mark, baker, Holt
Page William, yeoman, ditto
Plaford James, baker, ditto
Sales Charles, draper, ditto
Smith Joseph, clerk, ditto
Thompson Robert, yeoman, ditto
Waller William, patten-maker, Briston

Wm	Coke	Wod.
0	1	12
2	3	3

Horsford.

	Win.	Coke	Wod.
Mann John, farmer, Horsford			
Murray Richard, ditto, ditto			
Pratt Christmas, Horsham St. Faith's			
Savage Robert, yeoman, Horsford			
	4	4	8

Horsham St. Faith's.

	Win.	Coke	Wod.
Burcham John, farmer, Horsham St. Faith's			
Ewing Stephen, miller, ditto			
Goss John, dyer, ditto			
Goose Robert, farmer, ditto			
Lovick Samuel, yeoman, Hevingham			
Pratt Richard, farmer, Horsham St. Faith's			
	6	6	0

Horstead.

	Win.	Coke	Wod.
Barrett Robert, esq. Horstead			
Barrett Robert, jun. esq. ditto			
Batchelor Horatio, esq. ditto			
Hilling William, bricklayer, ditto			
Lee William, farmer, Carlton Rode			
Oakes William, ditto, Horstead			
Spooner Nash, yeoman, Coltishall			
Watts Henry Palmer, esq. Horstead			
	1	2	8

Hoveton St. John.

	Win.	Coke	Wod.
Blofield Thomas, esq. Hoveton St. John			
Cadge Michael, miller, ditto St. Peter			
Hall John, wheelwright, ditto St. John			
Lekee Peter, gent. Little Brand			
Piggin John, Blacksmith, Burlingham			
Piggin Robert, smith, Hoveton St. John			
Utting Charles, farmer, Carlton			
	0	0	7

Hoveton St. Peter.

	Win.	Coke	Wod.
Aufrere Anthony, esq. Hoveton St. Peter			
Negus Henry, esq. ditto			
Wells John, gent. Blofield			
	0	1	3

Houghton.—South Greenhoe.

	Win.	Coke	Wod.
Grief Jeremiah, yeoman, South Wootton			
	1	1	0

K

Houghton le Hole.

	Win.	Coke	Wod.
Harris Thomas, gent. Bacton			
Loose Isaac, farmer, Sharrington			
	1	1	1

Howe.

	Win.	Coke	Wod.
Arnold Richard, farmer, Howe			
Woolorton Edmund, ditto, Alburgh			
	0	1	2

Hunstanton.

	Win.	Coke	Wod.
Birkbeck John, gent. Hunstanton			
Cooke William, labourer, ditto			
Harrison Thomas, publican, Great Ringstead			
Norman Abraham, farmer, Hunstanton			
Pattern Michael, ditto, South Creak			
Pickrell John, ditto, Ringstead			
Pigman Richard, labourer, Hunstanton			
Russell Robert, farmer, Briningham			
	7	8	1

Hunworth.

	Win.	Coke	Wod.
Barber Robert, farmer, Felthorpe			
Cooke Thomas, miller, Hindringham			
Curtis Thomas, farmer, Hunworth			
Funnell Richard, cordwainer, ditto			
Funnell R. jun. land-surveyor, Hindringham			
Peck Richard, carpenter, Sharrington			
Swallow Charles, gunsmith, Hunworth			
Waller Thomas, charcoal-burner, ditto			
Weeds Richard, farmer, East Ruston			
	5	6	4

Holkham.

	Win.	Coke	Wod.
Coke Thomas William, esq. Holkham			
Crick Francis, gent. Fulmodestone			
Earl Thomas, labourer, Wells			
Farly William, groom, ditto			
Jones William, husbandman, ditto			
Kendall William, labourer, Hempton			
Savage Henry, carpenter, East Basham			
Sewell John, servant, Little Walsingham			
Wilkerson Thomas, ditto, Wells			
Woolnough Ben. publican, Burnham Overy			
	10	9	0

Illington.

	Win.	Coke.	Wod.
Gates Francis, farmer, Banham			
ellis George, ditto, Tibenham			
	0	0	2

Ingham.

	Win.	Coke.	Wod.
Comer Paul, shopkeeper, Stalham			
Croxton Cornelius, yeoman, Ingham			
Cubitt Benjamin, farmer, ditto			
Elsden Lazaret, bricklayer, ditto			
Florey William, yeoman, ditto			
Harvey John, farmer, ditto			
Leist Edward, ditto, ditto			
Long David, bricklayer, ditto			
Lusher John, yeoman, ditto			
Matthews John, miller, ditto			
Mitchell John, farmer, ditto			
Postle Robert, ditto, ditto			
Rust William, yeoman, ditto			
Salmon Philip, farmer, ditto			
Scott Daniel Durrant, esq. ditto			
Whaites Robert, gent. ditto			
Wagg William, publican, Worstead			
	5	6	12

Ingoldesthorpe.

	Win.	Coke.	Wod.
Benn Benjamin, farmer, Ingoldesthorpe			
Davey William, clerk, Anmer			
Davey William, jun. ditto, Ingoldesthorpe			
Raven John, esq. Massingham Magna			
	0	3	4

Ingworth.

	Win.	Coke.	Wod.
Ellis William, gent. Ingworth			
Randall William, yeoman, ditto			
	1	1	1

Intwood.

	Win.	Coke.	Wod.
Muskett Joseph, farmer, Intwood			
	1	1	0

Irstead.

	Win.	Coke.	Wod.
Bloom John, yeoman, Irstead			
Horner Leonard, farmer, ditto			
Joy John, ditto, ditto			
Roberts Peter, ditto, ditto			
	2	2	2

K 2

Islington.

	Win.	Coke.	Wod.
Cammack James, labourer, Tilney St. Law.			
Hardy John, glazier, Wiggenhall St. Ger.			
	1	1	1

Itteringham.

	Win.	Coke.	Wod.
Blyth Samuel, yeoman, Ingworth			
Jeckell Robert, blacksmith, Letheringset			
Plaford Thomas, carpenter, Itteringham			
Slipper James, ditto, ditto			

Kelling.

	Win.	Coke.	Wod.
Davey Joseph, farmer, Kelling			
Girdlestone William, clerk, ditto			
Girdlestone Zurishaddai, esq. ditto			
Winn James, yeoman, ditto			
	1	2	3

Kempston—Launditch.

	Win.	Coke.	Wod.
Chamberlin William, farmer, Wendling			
Johnson John, gent. Walpole St. Peter			
	1	1	3

Kenninghall.

	Win.	Coke.	Wod.
Barham William, farmer, Kenninghall			
Burlingham Francis, gent. ditto			
Brewster Robert, farmer, Garboldisham			
Briggs John, gardener, Kenninghall			
Cooke William, farmer, ditto			
Cooke Edmund, ditto, ditto			
Dudson Daniel, cordwainer, N. Buckenham			
Linstead Samuel, farmer, Kenninghall			
Mendham Isaac, ditto, ditto			
Osborn John, mason, Forncet St. Peter			
Palmer John, farmer, New Buckenham			
Reeve James, gent. Winfarthing			
Scott William, farmer, Sporle			
Wells Henry, miller, Banham			
West Edmund, carrier, Kenninghall			
Wilthy Thomas, labourer, ditto			
	2	2	0

Kerdiston.

	Win.	Coke.	Wod.
Cotton John, farmer, Kerdiston			
Eglinton John, ditto, Whitwell			
Lack John, ditto, Kerdiston			
Leeds Thomas, ditto, ditto			
	6	9	11

Kerdiston.

Lloyd Henry, gent. Bawdswell
Lloyd Guy, ditto, ditto
Neale Israel, farmer, Reepham

Kestwick.

Clarke Francis, farmer, Acle
Gurney Richard, esq. Keswick

Ketteringham.

Bates John, farmer, Wymondham
Futter John, ditto, Tharston

Kettlestone.

Cory James, clerk, Kettlestone
Dennis T. M. farmer, ditto
Jex Thomas, ditto, Little Snoring
Read Henry, jun. wheelwright, kettlestone

Kilverstone.

Wright John, gent. Kilverstone

Kimberley.

Cadywold Wm. Cockell, farmer, Attleburgh
Smith Jeremiah, ditto, Hardingham
Watson T. C. jun. ditto, Little Brand

Kirby Bedon.

L'Oste Joseph, clerk, Hainford
Mann Thomas, farmer, Kirby Bedon

Kirby Cane.

Clarke Tifford, farmer, Bedingham
Ingate William, blacksmith, Kirby Cane
Wilson George, clerk, Eccles
Wilson Henry, ditto, Kirby Cane
Wright Zachariah, farmer, Hackford

Kirstead.

Cooke Richard, farmer, Tivetshall St. Marg.
Kerrison Charles, ditto, Topcroft
Underwood John, ditto, Seething
Whall Robert, gent. Kirstead

Parish	Win.	Coke	Wod.
Kestwick	5	5	2
Ketteringham	2	2	0
Kettlestone	0	0	2
Kilverstone	4	4	0
Kimberley	0	0	1
Kirby Bedon	0	0	3
Kirby Cane	1	2	1
Kirstead	3	4	2
	2	2	2

Knapton.

Allison Thomas, yeoman, Knapton
Allison Joseph, ditto, ditto
Atkinson Charles, ———, ditto
Cooper John, yeoman, ditto
Collins John, farmer, Witton
Cornish Robert, carpenter, Knapton
Cook Stephen, clerk, Oulton
London Robert, gent. Knapton
Reynolds Joseph, yeoman, ditto
Watts Christmas, blacksmith, Marsham

Lammas.

Barton William, labourer, Lammas
Blofield Thos. Calthorpe, clerk, Felmingham
Bowman Clements, labourer, Lammas
Candler Philip, clerk, ditto
Damant William, esq. ditto
Goterson John, gent. Harpley
Lubbock William, esq. Lammas

Langmere.

Algar John, farmer, Langmere
Barber Benjamin, ditto, ditto
Burgess John, ditto, ditto

Langham.

Boyce Thomas, wheelwright, Langham
Frost Stephen, gent. ditto
Rush John, labourer, Field-dalling
Wells Cubit, farmer, Langham

Langley.

Ling Abraham, farmer, Langley
Proctor Sir Thomas B. bart. ditto
Read John, farmer, Loddon
Smith John, labourer, Langley

Larlingford.

Barker William, farmer, Larling
Cocksedge Samuel, victualler, ditto
Leech Philip, clerk, ditto

Parish	Win.	Coke	Wod.
Knapton	7	8	3
Lammas	5	6	2
Langmere	1	1	2
Langley	4	4	0
Larlingford	4	4	0
	0	2	3

Lessingham.

Bartram John, farmer, Lessingham
Balls John, ditto, Happisburgh
Cubitt Benjamin, ditto, Lessingham
Frary Thomas, ditto, ditto
Watts Augustine, ditto, ditto

Letheringset.

Burrell Nathaniel, surgeon, Letheringset
Burrell John, clerk, ditto
Cobon James, farmer, Holt
Cobon James, wheelwright, Letheringset
Hardy William, gent. ditto
Hardy William, jun. brewer, Southrepps
Lamb Charles, cordwainer, Letheringset
Newman Thomas, farmer, Sharrington
Rouse Peter, gent. Thornage
Rouse Richard, miller, Letheringset
Youngman Thomas, millwright, ditto

Letton.

Gurdon Thor. Phil. esq. Stow Bedon
Gurdon Theophilus, ditto, Letton
Norton Isaac, farmer, Stow Bedon
Stebbings Henry, ditto, Southbergh

Lexham East.

Burton William, farmer, East Lexham

Lexham West.

Back Edward, farmer, West Lexham
Durrant William, husbandman, ditto
Mays John, carpenter, ditto
Simons Robert, husbandman, ditto

Leziate.

Forster Thomas, gent. Letheringsett

Lingwood.

Ayres Richard, farmer, Lingwood
Dennison John, clerk, Loddon
Goddard Thomas, ditto, Lingwood
Goddard Erasmus, ditto, ditto

Place	Win.	Coke	Wod.
Lessingham	0	0	5
Letheringset	6	5	6
Letton	0	4	2
Lexham East	0	0	1
Lexham West	4	4	0
Lingwood	1	1	0

Lingwood.

Merrison James, husbandman, Lingwood
Norfor William, farmer, ditto
Read Thomas, ditto, ditto
Read Robert, ditto, ditto
Rust John, ditto, ditto

Limpenhoe.

Browning Benjamin, farmer, Limpenhoe
Fowler John, ditto, ditto
Jermyn James, ditto, Moulton
Maddison Browning, ditto, Limpenhoe
Mallett Peter, ditto, ditto

Litcham.

Carrington John, cooper, Litcham
Claxton John, cordwainer, Garvestone
Garner Henry, tailor, Litcham
Jarmyn Moody, aledraper, Foulden
Kennedy John, schoolmaster, Litcham
Kendall Joseph, blacksmith, ditto
Lynes John, maltster, ditto
Orvis William, farmer, Beeston
Raven Peter, surgeon, Litcham
Took John, cordwainer, ditto
Wodehouse the Hon. Armine, clerk, ditto

Loddon.

Britt Thomas, gent. Loddon
Brown Edmund, D. farmer, ditto
Clarke Samuel, whitesmith, ditto
Clarke John, wheelwright, ditto
Cole James, farmer, ditto
Cole John, ditto, ditto
Cole William, attorney, ditto
Cook William, farmer, ditto
Crisp William, ditto, ditto
Crisp John, bricklayer, ditto
Crickmer William, grocer, ditto
Dowson William, farmer, Shotesham
Devey Jonathan, bricklayer, Loddon
Fayerman John, clerk, ditto
Gilbert Thomas, gent. Chedgrave

Place	B in.	Coke	Wod.
Lingwood	6	8	3
Limpenhoe	5	3	1
Loddon	2	6	10

Loddon.

Hall John, baker, Loddon
Jollye Guyton, gent. ditto
Knapp Thomas, sen. gardener, ditto
Leamon William, linen-weaver, ditto
Plow John, cordwainer, ditto
Reynolds Thomas, shopkeeper, ditto
Rudrum John, innkeeper, ditto
Scarlet Philip, miller, ditto
Spurgeon William, publican, ditto
Ward John, collar-maker, ditto
Ward Robert, carpenter, ditto
White Thomas, ditto, ditto
Winter William, plumber, ditto

Longham.

Hastings Thomas, farmer, Longham
Hastings William, ditto, ditto
Kemp Thomas, husbandman, ditto
Winter Robert, cordwainer, ditto
Winter Thomas, blacksmith, ditto

Lopham North.

Beales Robert, farmer, North Lopham
Beales John, butcher, ditto
Bowell William, farmer, ditto
Carman Robert, ditto, ditto
Cook Nathaniel, ditto, South ditto
Coats William, linen-weaver, North ditto
Gooch John, ditto, ditto
Lovick John, ditto, ditto
Lovick William, ditto, ditto
Lorimer William, farmer, ditto
Ludbrooke William, linen-weaver, ditto
Mornement James, farmer, Garboldisham
Murton James, ditto, Blo Norton
Porter Samuel, gent. North Lopham
Pratt Stephen, farmer, South ditto
Rolfe John, ditto, North ditto
Rolfe William, ditto, ditto
Wharton George, sen. ditto, ditto
Wharton John, ditto, Garboldisham
Womack Thomas, ditto, North Lopham

Win.	Coke	Wod.
11	16	18
5	5	0

Lopham North.

Womack Micah, farmer, North Lopham
Worton George, ditto, South ditto
Worledge Robert, ditto, North ditto

Lopham South.

Corley Crispin, farmer, South Lopham
Cotton John, ditto, ditto
Doe John, drover, ditto
Fox John, whitesmith, Snetterton
Fox Thomas, esq. South Lopham
Gardiner Thomas, shopkeeper, ditto
Hassell Thomas, higler, ditto
Lovick Robert, farmer, ditto
Pratt John, ditto, ditto
Rye Francis, ditto, ditto
Soar Robert, ditto, ditto
Soar Jonathan, ditto, ditto
Thurlow Thomas, ditto, Old Buckenham
Wilby James, labourer, South Lopham

Ludham.

Crowe John H. gent. Yarmouth
Garrett James, farmer, Ludham
Harrison William, gent. Yarmouth
Harrison Roger, farmer, Ludham
Howes Daniel, wheelwright, Blofield
Johnson William C. farmer, Ludham
Page John B. ditto, Repps
Palgrave Isaac, yeoman, Ludham
Roll William, farmer, Hindringham
Runmons John, maltster, ditto
Slipper Thomas, farmer, Ludham
Smith Thomas, sen. shoemaker, Catfield
Smith Thomas, jun. ditto, ditto
Tann William, miller, Ludham
Ward Henry, innkeeper, ditto
Weeds Richard, farmer, East Ruston

Lynford.

Eyres George Robert, esq.

Win.	Coke	Wod.
11	15	12
4	6	11
7	9	10
0	1	1

Lyng.--- Eynsford.

Anson Henry, clerk, Oxnead
Anson Charles, ditto, Lyng
Hamerton John, gent. ditto
Smith Thomas, farmer, ditto
Smith John, ditto, Elsing
Spingall Thomas, ditto, Lyng

Lynn West.—Marshland.

Broadbent Thomas, merchant, West Lynn
Cooper William, farmer, ditto St. Peter
Crampton Stephen, ditto, West Lynn
Fisher Robert, gardener, ditto
Gagen Goddard, farmer, ditto St. Peter
Goddard George, butcher, West Lynn
Harris James, gent. ditto
Sessions Thomas, farmer, ditto
Tailor Joseph, cordwainer, ditto
Wardall Major, yeoman, ditto

Lynn.

Allen Wm. Green, master-mariner, K. Lynn
Allen John Maxey, esq. ditto
Allen William, grocer, ditto
Allen Thomas, esq. ditto
Allen Stephen, clerk, Houghton
Allen Stephen jun. ditto, Dunton
Andrews Joseph, grocer, King's Lynn
Ashby John Clarke, draper, ditto
Atto William, cabinet-maker, ditto
Ayre James, merchant, ditto
Ayre Thomas, ditto, ditto
Balding Samuel, woollen-draper, ditto
Bailey Martin, gardener, ditto
Banham John, butcher, East Rudham
Bagge Thomas Philip, esq. King's Lynn
Bagge Thomas, ditto, ditto
Bagge William, ditto, ditto
Bagge Henry Lee, banker, ditto
Baxter Benjamin, mariner, South Lynn
Bailey George, gent. ditto
Barrett Richard, victualler, King's Lynn
Bailey John, mariner, ditto

Win.	Coke	Wod.
3	5	3
9	9	1

Lynn.

Batterbee Benjamin, labourer, King's Lynn
Bartram John, butcher, ditto
Baker Thomas, baker, ditto
Baker Samuel, esq. ditto
Banyard Charles, farmer, East Dereham
Barry Samuel, yeoman, King's Lynn
Bangs Joshua, boatman, ditto
Bellard William, mariner, ditto
Beck Samuel, ditto, ditto
Best Jonathan, cabinet-maker, ditto
Bellamy Thomas, mariner, Burnham West.
Bigley Thomas, bricklayer, King's Lynn
Bird Joshua, cryer, ditto
Bird Robert, yeoman, ditto
Blencowe John Prescot, merchant, ditto
Bloy Henry, innkeeper, ditto
Blois William, meter, ditto
Bowker Alexander, esq. ditto
Boyce Francis, porter-dealer, ditto
Browne James, carpenter, ditto
Browne Daniel, draper, ditto
Brady Charles, dancing-master, ditto
Brereton Robert, peruke-maker, ditto
Browne Benjamin, stone-mason, ditto
Breame Thomas, gent. ditto
Brindley Thomas, ship-builder, ditto
Brook James, ironmonger, ditto
Brooks John, gent. ditto
Bunn Thomas, fisherman, ditto
Bunnett Samuel, schoolmaster, ditto
Burn Mark, clerk, ditto
Burlinson Thomas, gent. ditto
Bullard John, brewer, ditto
Cary John, gent. ditto
Carr William, cutler, ditto
Case William, esq. ditto
Cage William, shipwright, ditto
Cage Thomas, porter, ditto
Cive William, carpenter, ditto
Carr Thomas, merchant, ditto
Carter William, innkeeper Watlington
Chadwick Wm. merchant's clerk, K. Lynn

Lynn.

Name	Win.	Coke.	Wod.
Chapman John, publican, King's Lynn			
Clarke John, butcher, ditto			
Clifton William, grocer, ditto			
Coulcher Martin, clerk, Gaytonthorpe			
Coulton James, ditto, North Wootton			
Cooper William, ironmonger, King's Lynn			
Coates John, cooper, ditto			
Cooper Thomas, linendraper, ditto			
Coe Thomas, baker, ditto			
Codling George, cornmeter, ditto			
Cotton Robert Rix, grocer, ditto			
Cobb Christopher, carpenter, ditto			
Coward John, tinman, ditto			
Cooper William, butcher, ditto			
Crawforth James, surgeon, ditto			
Crowe Henry, sailmaker, ditto			
Crome Samuel, cordwainer, ditto			
Creak William, linen-draper, ditto			
Cummings George, cooper, ditto			
Curtis Benjamin, mariner, ditto			
Dawson John, baker, ditto			
Dawson John, ditto, ditto			
Daisley John, pilot, ditto			
Daisley Robert, tailor, ditto			
Dalton James, sawyer, ditto			
Davison Francis, carpenter, ditto			
Day Thomas, esq. ditto			
Davy James, watch-maker, ditto			
Danderson, John, baker, ditto			
Darsley John, waterman, ditto			
Denham William, merchant, ditto			
Dawson Daniel, cordwainer, ditto			
Depling Robert, porter, ditto			
Diamond Daniel, confectioner, ditto			
Dickenson Henry, gent. South Lynn			
Dickson Edward, sawyer, ditto			
Dillingham James, merchant, ditto			
Dixon John, grocer, ditto			
Dixon Thomas, victualler, West Winch			
Dow Thomas, gent. King's Lynn			
Docking William, carter, ditto			
Eagleton John, gent. Stoke			

Lynn.

Name	Win.	Coke.	Wod.
Ebden James, cork-cutter, King's Lynn			
Eccles William, tailor, ditto			
Edwards E. clerk, Terrington St. Clement			
Edwards John, esq. King's Lynn			
Eldridge Richard, stone-mason, ditto			
Elsden Edmund Rolfe, esq. ditto			
English John, merchant, ditto			
Everard Scarlet, esq. ditto			
Everard Edward, ditto, ditto			
Everard Edward, jun. esq. ditto			
Fake Thomas, mariner, ditto			
Falkner Henry, gent. ditto			
Fotherape Thomas, painter, ditto			
Fox Robert, cooper, ditto			
Franklin John, labourer, ditto			
Francis Robert John, clerk, Clenchwarton			
Fuller John, innkeeper, King's Lynn			
Fysh James, esq. ditto			
Fysh William, draper, ditto			
Galloway John, grocer, ditto			
Gagen Thomas, soap-boiler, ditto			
Garland William, mariner, ditto			
Garrod John, rope-maker, ditto			
Gent William, porter, ditto			
Goodwin Harvey, attorney, ditto			
Goodwin William, builder, ditto			
Goscar Thomas, plumber, ditto			
Griffin Robert, potter, ditto			
Green Robert, merchant, ditto			
Green Charles, parish clerk, South ditto			
Greeves John, currier, King's ditto			
Grant Valentine, innkeeper, ditto			
Gromitt Thomas, waiter, ditto			
Guggle Adam, mariner, ditto			
Gunner Thomas, glover, ditto			
Gunnell Thomas, fruiterer, ditto			
Guy Thomas, merchant, ditto			
Hales Robert, clerk, Hemsby			
Haws William, tailor, King's Lynn			
Hawkinson Robert, ditto, ditto			
Hawes Christopher, baker, ditto			
Harrison Thomas, plasterer, ditto			

Lynn.

	Win.	Coke	Wod.
Hardwick Edmund, cordwainer, King'sLynn			
Harris Charles, hair-dresser, ditto			
Haycock Abraham, ironmonger, ditto			
Haycock Robert, anchorsmith, ditto			
Harwood John, attorney, Tilney St. Law.			
Harwood William, labourer, King's Lynn			
Hardyman William, clerk, Shouldham			
Hadley Isagney, gent. King's Lynn			
Hemington John, esq. ditto			
Hendry John, bricklayer, ditto			
Headley Thomas, cordwainer, ditto			
Hill William, mariner, ditto			
Hogg Edward, esq. Wormegay			
Hogg George, jun. ditto, Thornham			
Hogg Fountaine, ditto, ditto			
Hook Robert, carpenter, King's Lynn			
Howlett Francis, ditto, ditto			
Howlett James, liquor-merchant, ditto			
Hornby Joseph, plumber, ditto			
Holland John, baker, ditto			
Howlett John, confectioner, ditto			
Hogg William, esq. Wormegay			
Hogg George, ditto, King's Lynn			
Hunter Robert, master-mariner, ditto			
Hubbard William, mariner, ditto			
Hunter Thomas, draper, ditto			
Hubbard John, mariner, ditto			
Hyllard Francis, baker, ditto			
Jackson William, merchant, ditto			
Jarvis Lewis Weston, attorney, ditto			
Jexon Thomas, cordwainer, Yarmouth			
Jewell George, mariner, King's Lynn			
Inkson George, butcher, ditto			
Inkson William, ditto, ditto			
Johnson George, gent. ditto			
Jordan William, grazier, ditto			
Judd John, shipwright, Wig. St. Mary M.			
Iveson Arthur, clerk, East Bradenham			
Kemball William, mariner, King's Lynn			
Keed John, hatter, ditto			
King William, bricklayer, ditto			
King Thomas, ditto, ditto			

Lynn.

	Win.	Coke	Wod.
Lake William, hatter, King's Lynn			
Lake William, machine-maker, ditto			
Laird William, mariner, ditto			
Lawrence Joseph, attorney, ditto			
Laird Benjamin, baker, ditto			
Langford William, druggist, ditto			
Lack John, farmer, South Creak			
Lack Daniel, gent. Gaywood			
Lindsey William, bricklayer, King's Lynn			
Liney Thomas, sail-maker, ditto			
Lockett John, glassman, ditto			
Lyther Benjamin, tailor, ditto			
Mayhew George, grocer,ditto			
Maw William, tinman, ditto			
Marshall Thomas, gardener, ditto			
Mattison John, victualler, Outwell			
Massingham T. chimney-sweeper, K. Lynn			
Marshall John, M. D. Terrington St. Clem.			
Manser Martin, master-mariner, K. Lynn			
Marshall John, mariner, ditto			
Mason John, hair-dresser, ditto			
Melvin Robert, gent. ditto			
Middleton John, merchant, ditto			
Mitchley Jonathan, carpenter, ditto			
Millington Samuel, mariner, ditto			
Middleton Barnard, surgeon, ditto			
Mowbray William, brush-maker, ditto			
Mugridge Thomas, cork-cutter, ditto			
Newman Charles, gent. ditto			
Newham Samuel, carpenter, ditto			
Newstead John, tailor, ditto			
Norton Elward, mariner, ditto			
Nurse Richarl, block-maker, ditto			
Oldmeadow James, cabinet-maker, ditto			
Oldmeadow Thomas, sen. furrier, ditto			
Oliver John, blacksmith, South ditto			
Overland Edward, porter, King's ditto			
Oxley Thomas, merchant, ditto			
Parlett William, draper, ditto			
Payne Thomas, salesman, ditto			
Pattle Samuel, innkeeper, South ditto			
Page Charles, cheese-factor, King's ditto			

	Win.	Coke	Wod.
Parfrement William, publican, King's Lynn			
Pettengall John, cordwainer, ditto			
Pearson Matthew, fisherman, ditto			
Peak George, grocer, ditto			
Pike William, carpenter, ditto			
Plowright Thomas, brazier, ditto			
Plumb William, harness-maker, ditto			
Porter James, ship-chandler, ditto			
Porter William, cordwainer, ditto			
Raby William, glover, ditto			
Raven Richard, painter, ditto			
Ravenshaw William, bricklayer, ditto			
Ravenshaw Peter, painter, ditto			
Reeve James, cabinet-maker, ditto			
Read John, basket-maker, ditto			
Register Henry, draper, ditto			
Redfearn Richard, M.D. ditto			
Richardson John, merchant's clerk, ditto			
Rishton Martin Folkes, esq. ditto			
Rodwell Robert, linen-draper, ditto			
Rollett William, sail-maker, ditto			
Rowlett Samuel, baker, ditto			
Roberts Nelson, cooper, ditto			
Rolling Richard, bricklayer, ditto			
Robertson Walter, esq. ditto			
Rogers William, farmer, Grimstone			
Rudram James, carpenter, Hockwold			
Rumball John, victualler, King's Lynn			
Sadd Stephen, shipwright, ditto			
Scott Isaac, fishmonger, ditto			
Self Lionel, gent. ditto			
Self Lionel, esq. ditto			
Sewell Clere, baker, ditto			
Sharp William Foster, corn-merchant, ditto			
Smith Henry, mariner, ditto			
Smith Henry, grocer, ditto			
Smith John, butcher, ditto			
Smith Thomas, merchant's clerk, ditto			
Smith William, grazier, ditto			
Smith Alexander, mariner, ditto			
Smith John, stable-keeper, ditto			
Smith Wainwright, sawyer, ditto			

M

	Win.	Coke	Wod.
Smith Alexander, anchorsmith, King's Lynn			
Sooley John, grocer, South Creak			
Spruce Francis, jobber, Tasburgh			
Spicer Thomas, fisherman, King's Lynn			
Spalding Richard, mariner, ditto			
Stockdale John, merchant, ditto			
Stockings John, cordwainer, ditto			
Stevens William, publican, ditto			
Sugars John, carpenter, ditto			
Swatman William, merchant, ditto			
Stoakham C. Molineux, bricklayer, ditto			
Swanson Griffin, gent. ditto			
Taylor T. Wilkinson, carpenter, ditto			
Taylor Joseph, esq. ditto			
Temple John, clerk, Ashwicken			
Thompson R. P. mariner, King's Lynn			
Thistle Charles, ditto, ditto			
Thetford Lynstead, carpenter, ditto			
Thorpe Robert, cooper, Stoke Ferry			
Tooke Sam. merchant's clerk, King's Lynn			
Tooke Wm. Carpenter, watch-maker, ditto			
Tooke Charles, carpenter, ditto			
Towell Richard, merchant, ditto			
Trappett William, cowman, ditto			
Trundle William, sadler, ditto			
Trundle Edmund, cordwainer, ditto			
Trundle John, ditto, ditto			
Tuck Edward, cooper, ditto			
Turner Robert Alderson, grocer, ditto			
Turner William, printer, ditto			
Twaites Edmund, baker, ditto			
Twaites Thomas, carter, ditto			
Upwood T. surgeon, Terrington St. Clement			
Wake Daniel, bricklayer, King's Lynn			
Wallard Francis, carpenter, ditto			
Wake Daniel, jun. ditto, ditto			
Walton Thomas, shopkeeper, ditto			
Walden James, mariner, ditto			
Watson Mark, ship-builder, ditto			
Watson Richard, bricklayer, ditto			
Watson Thomas, shipwright, ditto			
Wardell John, draper, ditto			

Lynn.

Win. | Coke | Wod.

Watson Robert, bricklayer, King's Lynn
Wales Joseph, ship-builder, ditto
Webster John, cordwainer, ditto
Welburn William, cork-cutter, ditto
Wells Thomas, ship-carpenter, ditto
Wethered William, draper, ditto
Whincop Robert, town-clerk, ditto
Whincop George Rayner, gent. ditto
Whitby James, carpenter, Whissonset
Winder William, clerk, Watton
Windett James, grocer, Kirstead
Wilkin John, cowkeeper, King's Lynn
Wilkinson Jacob, mariner, ditto
Wood Christopher, bricklayer, ditto
Woods Henry, carpenter, ditto
Wright Henry, publican, ditto
Young James, labourer, ditto
Young Thomas, cow-man, ditto

264 | 286 | 66

Mannington.

Oakes Thomas, farmer, Sloley

1 | 1 | 0

Marham.

Aylmer John, farmer, Marham
Bennett Robert, yeoman, ditto
Cousins Christmas, ditto, ditto
Makemead William, ditto, ditto
Parkinson John, tailor, Downham Market
Peter James, farmer, Wiggenhall St. Peter
Spruce Charles, ditto, Marham
Winearls William, jun. ditto, Yaxham
Winearls William, ditto, Marham
Witread John, yeoman, ditto

4 | 5 | 5

Marsham.

Cook George, bricklayer, Tuttington
Cook Joseph, carpenter, Marsham
Cutting John, yeoman, ditto
Everett William, esq. ditto
Elvin David, miller, ditto
Glatten James, yeoman, ditto
Robertson Alexander, grocer, ditto

M 2

Marsham.

Win. | Coke | Wod.

Soame Samuel, yeoman, Marsham
Smith Robert, cordwainer, ditto
Watts Joseph, yeoman, Itteringham
Wighton Charles, ditto, Marsham

7 | 7 | 6

Martham.

Bean James, farmer, Martham
Beyerly John, shoe-maker, ditto
Brownson William, husbandman, ditto
Bushel William, butcher, ditto
Carrier John, farmer, Rollesby
Creasy William, ditto, Martham
Davey William, blacksmith, ditto
Dixon Thomas, shoe-maker, ditto
Fairweather William, carpenter, ditto
Faulkner John, husbandman, ditto
Francis Thomas, farmer, ditto
Garnham William, shopkeeper, ditto
Hindle Nathaniel, plumber, Stalham
Humfrey Henry, farmer, ditto
Jeffries John G. surgeon, Martham
Linford William, husbandman, ditto
Pollard William, farmer, ditto
Pollard Charles, ditto, ditto
Porter Robert, ditto, ditto
Ransome Robert, husbandman, ditto
Rising Benjamin, farmer, ditto
Rising Thomas S. ditto, ditto
Rising Thomas, ditto, ditto
Seeley John, butcher, ditto
Vale Henry, gent. Yarmouth
Vincent Richard, wheelwright, Martham
Watson William, husbandman, ditto
Watson Clement, ditto, ditto
Wells William, miller, ditto
Wilson George, ditto, ditto
Warner Richard, farmer, ditto

6 | 13 | 23

Massingham Magna.

Beck William, yeoman, Cawston
Beck Anthony, farmer, ditto
Blyth William, ditto, Massingham Magna

Massingham Magna.

	Win.	Coke	Wod.
Hanno:1 Horace, clerk, North Walsham			
Hillings Robert, farmer, Massingham Magna			
Reynolds James, surgeon, ditto			
Wright William, carpenter, ditto	5	6	1

Massingham Little.

	Win.	Coke	Wod.
Mordaunt Charles, clerk, Massingham Parva			
Stanford Henry, farmer, Great Fransham	0	1	2

Matlask.

	Win.	Coke	Wod.
Booty William, gent. Matlask			
Gunton Dennis, esq. ditto			
Miller John, yeoman, ditto			
Nurse John, farmer, Waborne	1	1	4

Mattishall Heath.

Baldwin Richard, farmer, Brundall
Bishop Farmer, barber, Mattishall
Carter John, dissenting-minister, ditto
Carter Richard, publican, ditto
Carter John, grocer, ditto
Chamberlain Nicholas, farmer, ditto
Clarke William, ditto, ditto
Dawson William, ditto, Yarmouth
Eagling John, wheelwright, Wicklewood
Edwards William, farmer, Mattishall
Gaskin John, carpenter, ditto
Green Francis, farmer, ditto
Hubbard Stephen, plumber, ditto
Hudson Thomas, blacksmith, ditto
Jeary David, wool-comber, ditto
Leggatt Thomas, farmer, ditto
Lindsey William, maltster, ditto
Meale James, gent. ditto
Middleton William, thatcher, Southbergh
Norton Robert, baker, Mattishall
Norton Lindoe, farmer, ditto
Parke Edmund, husbandman, ditto
Petchell John, gent. ditto
Petchell John, farmer, ditto
Porter John, ditto, Whissonset
Smith William, ditto, Mattishall

Mattishall Heath.

	Win.	Coke	Wod.
Thorn Robert, surgeon, Mattishall			
Ward William, farmer, ditto.			
Webster William, bricklayer, ditto			
Wingfield Daniel, farmer, Mattishall Bergh			
Wright William, surgeon, Mattishall	6	7	26

Mattishall Bergh.

	Win.	Coke	Wod.
Edwards John, weaver, Mattishall Bergh			
Kerr Stephen, farmer, Mattishall			2
Perkins Simon, ditto, Mattishall Bergh			
Rouse Richard, ditto, ditto			
Steward William, ditto, ditto	3	4	

Mautby.

	Win.	Coke	Wod.
Pearce William, farmer, Yarmouth			
Pearce William, jun. ditto, ditto			
Pettingle William, ditto, West Somerton			
Rising Edward, ditto, Filby			
Womack Arthur, ditto, Runham	5	5	0

Melton Great.

	Win.	Coke	Wod.
Darby John, farmer, Great Melton			
Hill John, carpenter, ditto			
Lombe Sir John, bart. Melton			
Redhead Benjamin, farmer, Wymondham			
Vince John, ditto, ditto			
Willins James, clerk, Great Melton	4	4	2

Melton Little.

	Win.	Coke	Wod.
Heath Edward, farmer, Little Melton			
Palmer Thomas, ditto, ditto	1	1	1

Melton Constable.

	Win.	Coke	Wod.
Astley Sir J. H. bart. Melton Constable			
Stoughton William, gent. Wells	2	2	0

Mendham.

	Win.	Coke	Wod.
Poole John, draper, Mendham.			
Squire David, hostler, ditto			
Thurkettle Robert, carpenter, ditto			
Wilson James, whistler, Redenhall			
Wright John, gent. Mendham	3	4	2

Merton.

Stevens Nobbs, farmer, Attleborough

Methwold.

Bell John, labourer, Methwold
Boggers John, farmer, ditto
Bovill Thomas, ditto, ditto
Caney Edward, ditto, ditto
Clarke W. H. ditto, ditto
Coates William, ditto, ditto
Cock Abraham, ditto, ditto
Constable Charles, ditto, ditto
Constable John, carpenter, ditto
Flatt William, farmer, ditto
Flatt William, ditto, ditto
Flatt William, ditto, Feltwell
Flatt John, ditto, Methwold
Flatt Robert, ditto, ditto
Fuller Edmund, ditto, ditto
Gordon Abraham, labourer, ditto
Gordon Henry, farmer, ditto
Hewing Edward, ditto, ditto
Hewing John, ditto, Feltwell
Hopkins Thomas, bricklayer, Methwold
Howlett John, farmer, ditto
Horne Simon, ditto, ditto
King Robert, ditto, ditto
King James, aledraper, ditto
Miller Jeffery, farmer, ditto
Miller Thomas, labourer, ditto
Newton John, farmer, ditto
Newton John, jun. ditto, ditto
Porter William, ditto, ditto
Rolfe Thomas, ditto, ditto
Rolfe Richard, ditto, ditto
Runball Samuel, schoolmaster, ditto
Symonds John, labourer, ditto
Tibbett William, ditto, ditto
Wabe William, farmer, ditto
Wortley Thomas, ditto, ditto

	Win.	Coke	Wod.
Merton	1	0	1
Total	1	3	35

Metton.

Allison James, carpenter, Felbrigg
Critoph John, yeoman, Metton
Pells Samuel, ditto, Roughton
Smith John, farmer, Salthouse
Sturky James, ditto, Town Barningham

Middleton.

Back Henry, labourer, Great Snoring
Curle William, farmer, Middleton
Goodings Thomas, farmer, North Runcton
Killett William, clerk, Middleton
Lancaster John, farmer, Feltwell
Thompson Wm. horse-dealer, King's Lynn
Thompson Ambrose, farmer, Gt. Fransham
Thompson William, farmer, West Winch

Mileham.

Beare William, farmer, Mileham
Bridges Bilby, carpenter, Holne Hale
Bunn John, farmer, Lyng
Carrington Edward, gent, Elsing
Clarke John, ditto, Mileham
Davy John, esq. ditto
Head John, husbandman, ditto
Holley Edward, farmer, ditto
Padget John, ditto, Great Dunham
Smith William, miller, Mileham
Stroulger John, carpenter, ditto

Mintlyn.

Skippon John, farmer, Middleton

Morley St. Peter.

Bowles William, farmer, Alburgh
Burrell John, ditto, Wymondham
Carter John, ditto, Morley St. Peter
Clarke Charles, ditto, ditto
Matthews John, farmer, ditto

	Win.	Cok.	Wod.
Metton	5	3	0
Middleton	8	8	0
Mintlyn	7	8	5
Morley	1	1	0
Total	1	1	4

Morley St. Botolph.

	Win.	Coke	Wod.
Ayton James, farmer, Morley St. Botolph			
Curson Robert, ditto, ditto			
Curson Robert, ditto, Deopham	2	2	1

Morston.

	Win.	Coke	Wod.
Buck William, farmer, Foulsham			
Butter Henry, gent. Morston			
Farthing William, mariner, ditto	3	2	1

Morton.

	Win.	Coke	Wod.
Dunnell Barnard, innkeeper, Weston			
Harley Joseph, farmer, Garvestone			
Palmer John, ditto, Swannington	2	1	1

Moulton.—Depwade Hundred.

	Win.	Coke	Wod.
Wilson Edward, clerk, Carleton			

Moulton.—Walsham Hundred.

	Win.	Coke	Wod.
Atkins William, farmer, Moulton			
Bates Edward, ditto, ditto			
Betts William, ditto, ditto			
Boulton Benjamin, miller, ditto			
Boult George, farmer, Acle			
Buxton Benjamin, ditto, Moulton			
Collins William, ditto, ditto			
Edge James, ditto, ditto			
Futter William, shoemaker, ditto			
Gilbert Charles, farmer, ditto			
Hall William, ditto, ditto			
Hall John, ditto, Aslacton			
Howard Robert, ditto, Moulton			
Howard Samuel, ditto, Wickhampton			
Mere Richard, farmer, Wacton			
Miller John, ditto, Moulton			
Miller Jonas, ditto, ditto			
Moyse William, ditto, ditto			
Scott William, cordwainer, ditto			
Smith Robert, carpenter, ditto			
Smith Christopher, farmer, ditto			
Watling Robert, carpenter, ditto	0	1	1
	7	15	15

Mourningthorpe.

	Win.	Coke	Wod.
Aldred James, farmer, Alburgh			
Fryer Thomas, ditto, Mourningthorpe			
Goldsworth Salem, ditto, ditto			
Howes Thomas, clerk, Fritton			
Irby the Hon. Capt. Mourningthorpe			
Smith John, farmer, Carlton Rode	4	5	2

Mulbarton.

	Win.	Coke	Wod.
Beevor Miles, clerk, Mulbarton			
Turner James, farmer, ditto			
Turner John, ditto, ditto	0	2	3

Mundesley.

	Win.	Coke	Wod.
Bartram James, yeoman, Mundesley			
Barnard William, gent. ditto			
Starr Matthew, carpenter, Knapton	2	1	2

Mundford.

	Win.	Coke	Wod.
Chapman John, farrier, Northwold			
Clarke Thomas, carpenter, Mundford			
Griffin Charles, shopkeeper, ditto			
Griffin John, yeoman, Thetford			
Morley James, warrener, Hockwold			
Pymar William, gent. Mundford			
Rudland Thomas, labourer, ditto			

Mundham.

	Win.	Coke	Wod.
Caley Joseph, thatcher, Mundham			
Mayer Daniel, gent. ditto			
Tibenthem Thomas, publican, Seething			
Woodrow William, husbandman, Mundham	3	3	5

Narborough.

	Win.	Coke	Wod.
Allen William, clerk, Narborough			
Frith Philip, merchant, ditto			
Sutton Parker, innholder, Boughton	1	1	3

Narford.

	Win.	Coke	Wod.
Hubbard Edward, servant, Necton	1	1	2

Neatishead.

	Win.	Coke	Wod.
Beals Richard, farmer, Guestwick			
Beals Richard, ditto, ditto	0	1	1

Neatishead.

Clowes John, farmer, Halvergate
Cubitt William, ditto, Neatishead
Riches Thomas Neave, farmer, ditto
Smith Thomas, yeoman, ditto

	Win.	Coke	Wod.
	0	3	6

Necton.

Bunn Robert, wheelwright, G. Fransham
Bunn Francis, ditto, Tittleshall
Buscall John, farmer, Great Dunham
Dickenson William, ditto, Necton
Eldred Edward, ditto, Great Dunham
Farrow Edmund, ditto, Necton
Judd James, grocer, ditto
Mason William, esq. ditto
Mitchell John, miller, Holme Hale
Ollett Edmund, husbandman, Necton
Wright Edmund, farmer, ditto

	Win.	Coke	Wod.
	2	4	9

Needham.

Chalker Richard, farmer, Starston
Foulger James, husbandman, Needham
Goulder Robert, farmer, ditto
Lodge Joseph, ditto, ditto
Paske George, esq. Saxthorpe
Pratt James, gent. Needham
Stygall William, higler, ditto

	Win.	Coke	Wod.
	3	5	3

Newton St. Faith's.

Baley Cullum, thatcher, Newton St. Faith's
Clark Thomas, farmer, Walcot
Hewett Foulger, yeoman, Newton St. Faith's
Hickling Benjamin, farmer, Horsham ditto
Jones Thomas, farrier, Felthorpe
Woodcock Joseph, w. weaver, Newton St. F.

	Win.	Coke	Wod.
	6	6	0

Newton West.

Chapman Francis, yeoman, West Newton
Clarke Thomas, ditto, ditto
Crafer Henry, farmer, ditto
Weatherhead William, clerk, Shernborne

	Win.	Coke	Wod.
	4	4	0

Newton Flotman.

Drake John, farmer, Newton Flotman
Kersey Abraham, ditto, Braconash
Sendall J. publican, Saxlingham Nethergate
Slapp T. P. clerk, Shelfanger

	Win.	Coke	Wod.
	2	2	2

Northwold.

Bales John, farmer, Northwold
Barham Robert, miller, ditto
Bennett Joseph, husbandman, ditto
Briston Thomas, farmer, ditto
Caney Thomas, parish-clerk, ditto
Crane Thomas, farmer, ditto
Dent David, shopkeeper, ditto
Dye Thomas, collar-maker, ditto
Harvey Thomas, esq. ditto
Hunt John, bricklayer, ditto
King Joseph, farmer, Feltwell
Nurse John, cordwainer, Northwold
Pearman Joseph, farmer, ditto
Pooley John, ditto, Feltwell
Russell Thomas, gent. Northwold
Scales John, jun. farmer, ditto
Smith William, ditto, ditto
Thurold William, ditto, Attleburgh
Tompson William, ditto, Northwold
Towler William, ditto, Mattishall
Turner William, labourer, Northwold
Upton William, ditto, ditto
Waddington Thomas, D. D. ditto
Watcass William, farmer, ditto
Wilkin Samuel, blacksmith, ditto
Youngs John, jun. farmer, ditto
Young John, ditto, ditto

Norton Subcorse.

Casborne John Spring, clerk, Wymondham
Garwood John, farmer, Norton
Gooch Robert, gent. Norton Subcorse
Horth James, farmer, ditto
Littlewood Samuel, labourer, ditto
Scarlet John, farmer, Gissing
Scarlet James, ditto, Thurlton

	Win.	Coke	Wod.
	1	2	26

Norton Subcorse.

Name	Win.	Coke	Wod.
Shaddelow Edward, gent. Norton Subcorse			
Tailor Robert, butcher, ditto	4	3	7
Warner William, shopkeeper, ditto			

Norwich.

Name	Win.	Coke	Wod.
Abbotts John, tailor, East Dereham			
Adkin Lancaster, D. D. Candley			
Amond Edward, labourer, Wymondham			
Anguish George, clerk, Moulton			
Angell John, currier, Lingwood			
Alderson Robert, esq. Yarmouth			
Athow Robert, gent. Hindringham			
Barnes John, whitesmith, Stratton St. Mary			
Barnard Thomas, gent. Diss			
Barrow Isaac, ditto, Alpington			
Bailey William, ditto, Cromer			
Basey John, yeoman, Marsham			
Baseley John Greene, esq. Belaugh			
Beevor John, M. D. Marham			
Beevor Hen. (Lakenham) ditto, Hackford			
Beevor James, esq. Catton			
Beare William, cordwainer, Great Snoring			
Bell John, cabinet-maker, Blickling			
Beckwith Thomas, clerk, Trunch			
Bidwell Rich. sack-manufacturer, Felthorpe			
Bird Bailey, gent. Tharston			
Blake Thomas, esq. Horstead			
Blofield John, throwsterer, Newton St. F.			
Bowman John, clerk, Poringland			
Boyce James, attorney, Catton			
Bradford Miles, gent. Wymondham			
Browne Robert Ives, esq. Methwold			
Browne James, cordwainer, Stratton St. M.			
Browne John, esq. Hetherset			
Browne Michael, clerk, Worstead			
Brown Crisp, merchant, Yarmouth			
Buck John, baker, Forncet St. Peter			
Buddry Anthony, grocer, South Walsham			
Burch Stephen, porter, Ringland			
Burrows William, grocer, Saxlthorpe			
Carr William, cordwainer, Attleborough			
Catermoul Thomas, gent. Yarmouth			

Norwich.

Name	Win.	Coke	Wod.
Carrington Henry, clerk, Billingford			
Chase William, liquor-merchant, Yarmouth			
Chamberlin Peter, esq. Tharston			
Chambers Nethercoat, gent. Needham			
Chapman Chas. John, clerk, Deopham			
Clarke Robert, carpenter, Aylmerton			
Clabburn Thomas, w. weaver, Tasburgh			
Coe John, broker, Bawdeswell			
Cocks Daniel, blacksmith, Thorpe			
Cooper Stephen, bricklayer, Panxworth			
Colman Edward, surgeon, Bressingham			
Coleman Henry, weaver, Dickleburgh			
Cooper J. F. law-stationer, Wymondham			
Coulson John, weaver, Newton St. Faith's			
Cousins John, leather-cutter, N. Walsham			
Colombine Paul, D. D. Thurlton			
Crowe James, (Lakenham) esq. Saham Toney			
Culley Richard, grocer, Fundenhall			
Cullington John, publican, Yarmouth			
Cullington Jas. (Lakenham) gent. Downham			
Day John, esq. Hapton			
Day Richard, clerk, Panxworth			
Day Starling, esq. Hockering			
Day Starling, jun. ditto, ditto			
Dalrymple William, Surgeon, Bawburgh			
Davey Jonathan, (Eaton) esq. Sprowston			
Daines James, merchant, Catton			
Deacon John, clerk, East Carlton			
Decker Thomas, clerk, Fundenhall			
De Hague Elisha, gent. Brundall			
Denmark William, farmer, Sprowston			
Decaux William, gent. Bawdeswell			
Dickins Mark H. esq. Gressenhall			
Digby John, gent. Stoke Holy Cross			
Dove Thomas, carpenter, Stratton St. Mary			
Dring John, miller, Easton			
Duckett William, publican, Little Melton			
Earl Charles, shopkeeper, Wymondham			
Eaton Thomas, silk-mercer, East Carlton			
Eagling Robert, cordwainer, Great Snoring			
Edgar Henry, esq. Oxwick			
Edwards Samuel, publican, Tasburgh			

Norwich.

	Win.	Coke	Wod.
Elwin Caleb, clerk, Booton			
Engledew William, dyer, Elsing			
Etheridge Philip, ironmonger, Starston			
Ewen Thomas Glover, esq. Hingham			
Fitch Joseph, chemist, Catton			
Foster William, jun. attorney, Easton			
Foster William, attorney, ditto			
Forster Richard, (Eaton) gent. Attleburgh			
Fox William, carpenter, Strumpshaw			
Francis Henry, attorney, East Carlton			
Fulcher James, gent. Filby			
Ganning Daniel, esq. Morley St. Botolph			
Gee Benjamin, farmer, Newton St. Faith's			
Goose Robert, ditto, Saxlingham			
Goodrum Godfrey, gent. Redenhall			
Gostling Francis, merchant, Plumstead Great			
Greeves Thomas, gent. Drayton			
Gurney John, (Earlham) esq. Costessey			
Gurney Joseph, (Lakenham) ditto, Cromer			
Hayton William, shopkeeper, Blofield			
Halton John, publican, Yarmouth			
Hansell Peter, clerk, Catton			
Harvey Robert, esq. Stoke Holy Cross			
Harvey Robert, jun. ditto, ditto			
Hannant Thomas, bargeman, Hindolveston			
Hancock Thomas Wiggs, clerk, Wendling			
Hall Henry, gent. Gressenhall			
Herring John, esq. Thurton			
Herring John, jun. merchant, Bale			
Hodds James, gent. Costessey			
Howes Thomas, clerk, Mourningthorpe			
Howes Gordon, gent. Moulton			
Hooke Edmund, esq. Mulbarton			
Howard John, gent. Sloley			
Hudson James, esq. Fincham			
Hutcheson Mich. publican, Newton Flotman			
Johnson John, gent. Waborne			
Johnson B. liquor-merchant, East Carlton			
Jones David, gent. Yarmouth			
Ives Jeremiah, (Town Close) clerk, Corpusty			
Kerrison Thomas Allday, esq. Loddon			
Kenney Edmund, gent. Shouldham			

Norwich.

	Win.	Coke	Wod.
Kett Henry, ditto, Dickleburgh			
Landy James, gent. Bunwell			
Lane Nicholas, mason, Shelton			
Lake William, cordwainer, Holt			
Leman Barnabas, esq. Yarmouth			
Leman Abraham, grocer, Gresham			
Limmer Samuel, yeoman, Bawdeswell			
Lincoln John, steward, Attleburgh			
Linley Ozias, T. clerk, Tharston			
Lowden John, sen. butcher, Acle			
Lowden John, jun. ditto, ditto			
Lowe William, smith, Smalburgh			
Lutbock Richard, M. D. Sculthorpe			
Matchett Jonathan, printer, Pulham Market			
Marsh Robert, gent. Brundall			
Martin Robert, aledraper, Thorpe			
Marsh James, esq. Dickleburgh			
Martineau Philip, surgeon, Trowse Newton			
Massingham John, gent. Little Bittering			
Meek James, glazier, Hempnall			
Merriman Jonathan, surgeon, Stalham			
Millard Charles Freeman, clerk, Hickling			
Millard Chas. (Bracondale) do. Trowse New.			
Morse John, esq. Toft Monks			
Moss Richard, ditto, Westfield			
Newton James Williams, clerk, Alderford			
Nichols Henry, farmer, Sprowston			
Nichols James, manufacturer, East Dereham			
Noverre Francis, gent. Yarmouth			
Parr Robert, clerk, Wymondham			
Palmer William, grocer, Tharston			
Page Joseph, gent. Stratton St. Michael			
Patteson John, M. P. Thorpe			
Patteson John Staniforth, esq. ditto			
Partridge Robert, ditto, Northwold			
Peek John, gent. South Walsham			
Peck William, aledraper, Newton St. Faith's			
Pightling William, merchant, Coltishall			
Plumtre Robert, esq. Cantley			
Pointer Henry, barber, Acle			
Prentice Samuel, quartermaster, Yarmouth			
Preston George, clerk, Beeston St. Lawrence			

Norwich.

	Win.	Coke	Wod.
Tompson Jas. Browne, clerk, Shropham			
Tompson Thomas, merchant, Yarmouth			
Tompson Timothy, esq. Great Witchingham			
Trafford Sigismund, esq. Enneth			
Unthank William, gent. Sprowston			
Ward John, baker, Shelton			
Watson Richard, farrier, Tasburgh			
Wagstaffe John, miller, Bawburgh			
Walker John, clerk, Stoke Holy Cross			
Weston Miles, esq. Mattishall Bergh			
Webb John Barton, gent. Diss			
West John, linen-draper, Aylsham			
Wegg George, labourer, Upton			
Webster Stephen, clerk, Claxton			
Wilch John, baker, Thorpe			
Wells John, gent. Coltishall			
Whittingham Paul, clerk, Martham			
Wicks Thomas, (Eaton) farmer, Felthorpe			
Woodcocke Richard, gent. Morton			
Wright Henry, plasterer, Erpingham			
	129	132	105

Oby.

	Win.	Coke	Wod.
Bathurst Henry, clerk, Oby			

Ormesby.

	Win.	Coke	Wod.
Barker Robert, husbandman, Yarmouth			
Bell William, gent. ditto			
Boutell Charles, clerk, Ormesby			
Clarke John, husbandman, ditto			
Clowes John, farmer, ditto			
Cooper William, ditto, South Walsham			
Fellowes Timothy, esq. Ormesby			
Goodwin John, blacksmith, ditto			
Manning William, esq. ditto			
Manship William, farmer, ditto			
Page Thomas, jun. carpenter, ditto			
Page Thomas, sen. bricklayer, ditto			
Price Eli Morgan, D. D. Yarmouth			
Read Robert, farmer, Ormesby			
Salmon Benj. Wimberley, clerk, Caister			
Symonds James, gent. Ormesby			
Shimpling James, carpenter, ditto			
	0	0	1

Norwich.

	Win.	Coke	Wod.
Priest John Fox, druggist, Lammas			
Purdy Robert, gent. Tunstead			
Raven John, esq. Whissonset			
Riches H. (Lakenham) servant, Poringland			
Ringer Edward, leather-cutter, Wymondham			
Roach Richard, plumber, Hevingham			
Robinson Thomas, gent. New Buckenham			
Salmon Richard, tailor, Hempton			
Scott John, gent. Diss			
Scott John, esq. Syderstrand			
Seamans John, butcher, Tasburgh			
Sieley Andrew, esq. Walcot			
Shalders William, leather-cutter, Catfield			
Shalders Richard, currier, Worstead			
Short William, carpenter, Acle			
Shrimplin D. throwster, Saxlingham N.			
Simpson William, attorney, Aylsham			
Smith Richard, brewer, Aslacton			
Smith John Charles, gent. Tibenham			
Smith James, grocer, Blofield			
Spark Robert, innkeeper, Hevingham			
Springall Edward, labourer, Heydon			
Springfield John, broker, Yarmouth			
Springfield Daniel, publican, Acle			
Springfield T. O. watch-maker, Yarmouth			
Springfield Edmund, shopkeeper, ditto			
Starkey Robert, gent. Coleby			
Stacey George, druggist, Tasburgh			
Sterling J. P. esq. East Dereham			
Staff Edward, gent. Easton			
Steward John, attorney, East Carlton			
Stone Thomas, gent. Wymondham			
Starkey Charles, ditto, Smalburgh			
Stannard Joseph, builder, Shotesham All St.			
Stoughton Thomas, gent. Heveringland			
Sudbury Thomas, dyer, Old Buckenham			
Suffield George, gent. Langley			
Sutton Charles, D. D. Thornham			
Taylor William, sen. esq. Diss			
Taylor William, jun. ditto			
Tawell Thomas, ditto, Attleborough			
Thurlow Edw. South, clerk, East Carlton			

Ormesby.

	Win.	Coke	Wod.
Skoyles Samuel, wheelwright, Ormesby			
Scrimer Robert, farmer, Rollesby			
Teasdale Peter, carpenter, Ormesby			
Tungate John, farmer, ditto			
Taylor Christopher, clerk, ditto			
Waters John, farmer, ditto			
Wooiston John, ditto, ditto			
	7	10	16

Overstrand.

	Win.	Coke	Wod.
Howes Joseph, yeoman, Trunch			
Wright Samuel, thatcher, Cromer			
	1	2	1

Ovington.

	Win.	Coke	Wod.
Chapman John, farrier, Rockland St. Peter			
Cook William, ditto, Ovington			
Francis John, cordwainer, ditto			
Hipkin Samuel, farmer, Hingham			
Lincoln Edmund, ditto, ditto			
Thompson John, ditto, ditto			
Whistler James, ditto, ditto			
	2	2	5

Oulton.

	Win.	Coke	Wod.
Cook Thomas, farmer, Foulsham			
Glasspoole Thomas, gent. Loddon			
Roe Thomas, farmer, Yarmouth			
Smith James, ditto, Holt			
	0	1	4

Outwell.

Boyce Robert, cooper, Outwell
Briggs John, shoe-maker, ditto
Goulding William, carpenter, ditto
Hardwick William, clerk, ditto
Hawkins Thomas, farmer, Upwell
Hamond Matthew, ditto, Outwell
Mote Thomas, carpenter, ditto
Neale Thomas, baker, ditto
Rate Francis, farmer, ditto
Thomson Thomas, victualler, ditto
Tiffin Robert, farmer, ditto
Trower Wm. collector of tolls, King's Lynn
Trott Matthew, farmer, Outwell
Trott John, ditto, ditto

Outwell.

	Win.	Coke	Wod.
Trott John, jun. farmer, Outwell			
Tomlinson John, ditto, ditto			
Truman Isaac, ditto, ditto			
Walton Robert, ditto, ditto			
Wells James, ditto, ditto			
Wilebore John, gent. Upwell			
Young Thomas, victualler, Outwell			
	12	13	10

Oxnead.

	Win.	Coke	Wod.
Hannant Richard, labourer, Oxnead			
Repton John, esq. Sloley			
	2	2	0

Oxwick.

	Win.	Coke	Wod.
Baker Thomas, farmer, Oxwick			
	1	1	0

Palgrave.

	Win.	Coke	Wod.
Kerrison Charles, esq. Wreningham			
Howes Thomas, farmer, Diss			
	0	0	2

Palling.

	Win.	Coke	Wod.
Crowe Robert, yeoman, Palling			
Crowe James, farmer, ditto			
Ditcham James, ditto, ditto			
Empson James, ditto, Smalburgh			
Howard Thomas, ditto, Palling			
	0	0	5

Punxworth.

	Win.	Coke	Wod.
England George, shoe-maker, Panxworth			
Heath Robert, esq. ditto			
Wells Benjamin, farmer, ditto			
	2	1	2

Paston.

	Win.	Coke	Wod.
Cremer Francis, farmer, Paston			
Curtis John, ditto, Catfield			
Gaze Thomas, ditto, North Walsham			
Howard Samuel, miller, Paston			
Rising John, farmer, Lynn			
Suffolk William, ditto, Paston			
	2	3	4

Pensthorpe.

	Win.	Coke	Wod.
Gwynn Richard, farmer, Fakenham			
	1	1	0

Pentney.

	Win.	Coke	Wod.
Carter Samuel, farmer, Pentney			
Lloyd John, esq. ditto			
Winch John, farmer, West Winch	0	0	3

Pickenham North.

	Win.	Coke	Wod.
Nave John, farmer, Holme Hale	0	0	1

Pickenham South.

	Win.	Coke	Wod.
Mills Edward, farmer, Shimpling	0	1	1

Plumstead Great.

	Win.	Coke	Wod.
Atwood John, farmer, Brockdish			
Gamble John, ditto, Plumstead			
Maidstone R. husbandman, Great Plumstead			
Maidstone William, ditto, ditto			
Minister James, carpenter, Brockdish	3	3	2

Plumstead Little.

	Win.	Coke	Wod.
Bullock Peter, farmer, Great Plumstead			
Kerrison John, ditto, Ranworth			
Leigh William, clerk, Little Plumstead			
Saul Benjamin, farmer, ditto			
Wigg Bernard, ditto, ditto	4	4	1

Poringland Great.

	Win.	Coke	Wod.
Riches John, husbandman, Poringland			
Smith James, farmer, ditto			
Utting Henry, innkeeper, Alpington	3	3	0

Potter Heigham.

	Win.	Coke	Wod.
Applegate Thomas, farmer, Potter Heigham			
Blaxell John, ditto, ditto			
Bower Robert, ditto, ditto			
George Henry, ditto, ditto			
Randall Timothy, yeoman, ditto			
Ransome Robert, farmer, Hickling			
Slipper John, gent. Potter Heigham			
Thaxter Samuel Davey, farmer, ditto			
Vincent Charles, miller, Catfield	2	2	7

Pulham.

	Win.	Coke	Wod.
Algar Robert, farmer, Pulham St. Mary			
Bentfield Joseph, ditto, Tivetshall St. Mary			
Browne William, ditto, Pulham Market			
Blomfield Benjamin, ditto, Bedingham			
Bowen Thomas, clerk, Pulham St. Mary			
Chenery John, farmer, Pulham Market			
Cole John, gent. Stratton St. Mary			
Cole William, farmer, Pulham Market			
Cunningham Tim. gent. Pulham St. Mary			
Drane Thomas, farmer, ditto			
Dunn James, ditto, ditto			
Fuller Daniel, ditto, Banham			
Hardy Jacob, ditto, Pulham St. Mary			
Howe Robert, carpenter, Wacton			
Jeffries John, blacksmith, Pulham Market			
Knight Geo. farmer, Pulham St. Mary Mag.			
Knights Daniel, ditto, Hardwick			
Knights Thomas, ditto, Pulham Market			
Manclarke P. Austin, esq. Pulham St. Mary			
Mills Ebenezer, surgeon, ditto			
Page Edmund, farmer, Pulham Market			
Parkerson Jas. gent. Pulham St. Mary Mag.			
Ray Thomas, farmer, ditto			
Self Robert, ditto, Pulham Market			
Sheldrake John, ditto, ditto			
Skipper Henry, publican, Pulham St. Marg.			
Smith J. C. farmer, Pulham St. Mary Mag.			
Theobald Jonathan, ditto, Yarmouth			
Webb William, gent. Pulham	8	9	21

Quarles.

	Win.	Coke	Wod.
Heagren Edmund, farmer, North Creak	1	1	0

Rackheath.

	Win.	Coke	Wod.
Davey John, farmer, Halvergate			
Davey Christopher, ditto, Rackheath			
Stracey Edward, esq. ditto	0	2	3

Rainham West.

	Win.	Coke	Wod.
Gunton George, wheelwright, W. Rainham	0	0	1

Rainham South.
Money Charles, farmer, Stibbard
Whiteman John, ditto, Gressenhall

Ranworth.
Browne William, farmer, Ranworth
Carver Thomas, ditto, ditto
Cuttin William, pump-maker, ditto
Free John, farmer, ditto
Free John, jun. ditto, ditto
Kerrison Matthias, ditto, ditto
Liest John, ditto, ditto
Skipper John, ditto, ditto
Townshend Robert, husbandman, ditto

Win.	Coke	Wod.
1	2	0

Raveningham.
Bacon Sir Edmund, bart. Raveningham
Banham Benjamin, farmer, ditto
Denny James, ditto, Thurlton
Fisher John, ditto, Hales
Playford Henry, ditto, Hardley
Rushmore Thomas, ditto, Toft Monks

Win.	Coke	Wod.
8	4	5

Redenhall.
Bardwell T. H. farmer, Redenhall
Browne William, ironmonger, ditto
Buxton John, farmer, Bedingham
Cotton Richard, gardener, Redenhall
Darby Robert, gent. ditto
Dowling Jeremiah, whitesmith, ditto
Edwards Lee, gardener, ditto
Holmes John, clerk, ditto
Hostler James, gardener, ditto
Kerrich John, esq. Mendham
Leatherdale Richard, hosier, Redenhall
Lovick J. W. innkeeper, ditto
Mean James, collar-maker, ditto
Taylor Thomas, gent. Forncet St. Peter
Tricker Robert, ditto, Redenhall
Shipton James, butcher, Starston
Symonds Charles, blacksmith, Mendham
Vipond John, carpenter, Redenhall
Websdale Charles, husbandman, Wortwell
Wright Jonathan, blacksmith, Redenhall

Win.	Coke	Wod.
0	0	6
7	12	13

Reedham.
Cockerill Daniel, butcher, Reedham
Johnson Jonathan, husbandman, ditto
Johnson Jonathan, labourer, ditto
Layton Charles, esq. ditto

Win.	Coke	Wod.
2	1	3

Reepham.
Breeze James, gardener, Whitwell
Franklin Peter, collar-maker, Reepham
Keeler Joseph, thatcher, Wood-dalling
Leeds Clement, cooper, Reepham
Symonds John, watch-maker, Thwaite
Wymer George, gent. Reepham

Win.	Coke	Wod.
3	4	4

Repps with Bastwick.
Belson Richard, farmer, Repps
Boyce Thomas, glazier, ditto
Dale Robert, farmer, ditto
Gilbert Samuel, husbandman, ditto
Nicholson William, ditto, ditto

Win.	Coke	Wod.
4	4	1

Repps North.
Bartram Robert, yeoman, Northrepps
Bird James, farmer, Holt
Carter John, yeoman, Southrepps
Cross John, ditto, Northrepps
Emery James, ditto, ditto
Pearson James, ditto, ditto
Starling Samuel, ditto, ditto

Win.	Coke	Wod.
5	4	3

Repps South.
Baker John, gent. Southrepps
Bartram Thomas, draper, ditto
Carter Edmund, baker, ditto
Cubitt John, clerk, Ridlington
Glover George, ditto, ditto
Harris William, gent. Syderstrand
Hewitt William, yeoman, Southrepps
Sago Robert, ditto, ditto
Shepherd Thomas, ditto, ditto

Reymerstone.
Durrant Gregory, husbandman, Gawestone
Filby John, farmer, Reymerstone

Win.	Coke	Wod.
4	4	6

Riston.

	Win.	Coke	Wod.
Chapman John, yeoman, Denver			
Pratt Edward Roger, esq. Riston	2	2	0

Rockland St. Mary.— Henstead Hun.

	Win.	Coke	Wod.
Andrews John, farmer, Rockland			
Blake Benjamin, blacksmith, ditto			
Crowe T. B. farmer, ditto			
Haywood John, ditto, ditto			
Howard John, ditto, Southbergh			
Hurne James, labourer, Rockland			
Parker John, ditto, ditto			
Parker John, ditto, ditto			
Rogers William, carpenter, ditto			
Thurston Robert, labourer, ditto	11	10	1

Rockland All Saints.

	Win.	Coke	Wod.
Springall William, weaver, Rockland All St.			
Towler John, farmer, Great Ellingham			
West Wm. shopkeeper, Rockland All St.	2	0	2

Rockland St. Andrew.

	Win.	Coke	Wod.
Chapman James, higler, Rockland St. An.			
Reynolds Robert, farmer, Rockland All St.			
Salter Thomas, ditto, Rockland St. Andrew			
Watling William, butcher, Rockland St. P.			

Rockland St. Peter.

	Win.	Coke	Wod.
Baldry Edward, farmer, Moulton			
Bowers Henry, ditto, Rockland St. Peter			
Carver Robert carpenter, ditto			
Cockell William, weaver, ditto			
Fielding James, cooper, Little Ellingham			
Hotson Benjamin, victualler, Caston			
Leech John, farmer, Rockland St. Peter			
Muskett Benjamin, ditto, ditto	2	2	2

Rollesby.

	Win.	Coke	Wod.
Annison Edward, thatcher, Rollesby			
Appleton Samuel, blacksmith, ditto			
Baker Thomas, clerk, ditto			
Collins Edward, shoe-maker, ditto	6	0	8

Reymerstone.

	Win.	Coke	Wod.
Gunton James, farmer, Reymerstone			
Hall Matthew, ditto, ditto			
High John, gent. ditto,			
Jessup John, farmer, ditto			
Lock William, ditto, Hingham			
Lock Dixon, ditto, Reymerstone			
Palmer John, farmer, ditto			
Pond Jarrett, ditto, ditto			
Vincent Timothy, butcher, ditto			
White John, shopkeeper, ditto	6	11	6

Rainthorpe.

	Win.	Coke	Wod.
Gay John, esq. Flordon	1	1	0

Riddlesworth.

	Win.	Coke	Wod.
Bevan Silvanus, esq. Riddlesworth			
Wake Baldwin, clerk, ditto	1	1	1

Ridlington.

	Win.	Coke	Wod.
Amis Abraham, miller, Ridlington			
Atkins William, farmer, ditto			
Banyard William, yeoman, Aylmerton			
Harris Nathaniel, plumber, Ridlington			
Howes Robert, farmer, Brunstead			
Nash Samuel, ditto, Wramplingham			
Wiseman William, ditto, Bacton	1	1	6

Ringland.

	Win.	Coke	Wod.
Blyth Matthew, wheelwright, Ringland			
Browne David, bricklayer, ditto			
Culley John, farmer, ditto			
Leggatt William, yeoman, ditto			
Leggatt William, ditto, ditto			
Palmer George, blacksmith, ditto	5	5	1

Ringstead.

	Win.	Coke	Wod.
Beany John, labourer, Stanhoe			
Bond William, farmer, Ringstead			
Stocking Henry, ditto, ditto			
Warren John, gent. ditto	4	4	0

Rollesby.

	Win.	Coke	Wod.
Crane Isaac, gardener, Rollesby			
Dye Isaac, farmer, ditto			
Docking George, ditto, Beighton			
Docking Abraham, ditto, Lingwood			
Dunham Harmer, ditto, Rollesby			
Fodder Wm. sen. husbandman, Yarmouth			
Harris James, ditto, Acle			
Kemp Robert, farmer, Rollesby			
Mapes Edmund, esq. ditto			
Miles Francis, blacksmith, ditto			
Miles James, farmer, ditto			
Palmer Samuel, husbandman, ditto			
Ransome John, farmer, ditto			
Russells Arthur, cordwainer, ditto			
Slaughter John, husbandman, ditto			
Sowells Daniel, farmer, ditto			
Sowells Thomas, gent. Burgh			
Watts Martin, gent. Rollesby	2	3	19

Rougham.

	Win.	Coke	Wod.
Barton William, farmer, Rougham			
Barton John, ditto, ditto			
Whaites John, ditto, ditto	2	3	1

Roughton.

	Win.	Coke	Wod.
Caston Robert, schoolmaster, Repps South			
Flaxman William, yeoman, Roughton			
Green John, glover, ditto			
Joy Edward, miller, Irstead			
Pile Robert, blacksmith, West Beckham	4	4	1

Roxham.

Narburn Thomas, farmer, Denver

Roydon.—Diss Hundred.

	Win.	Coke	Wod.
Annis John, farmer, Roydon			
Dye John, ditto, ditto			
Elliott William, ditto, ditto			
Frere John, esq. ditto			
Good Charles, husbandman, ditto			
Hinchley John, farmer, ditto			
Kitchen William, ———, Diss	1	1	0

P 2

Roydon.—Diss Hundred.

Mullinger Thomas, mole-catcher, Roydon
Smith John, linen-weaver, ditto
Warne Thomas, husbandman, ditto

Roydon.—Freebridge Lynn Hund.

	Win.	Coke	Wod.
Burrell Henry, jun. farmer, Roydon			
Lynn James, gent. ditto			
Pung Robert, farmer, ditto	0	3	10

Rudham East.

	Win.	Coke	Wod.
Barker Francis, labourer, East Rudham			
Dewing Richard, farmer, Walpole St. Peter			
Drage John, shopkeeper, East Rudham			
Hilden John, labourer, ditto			
Mays Richard, publican, ditto			
Powell John, smith, ditto			
Rathbone Richard, labourer, ditto			
Tipple William, ditto, ditto			
Young John, farmer, King's Lynn	3	3	0

Rudham West.

	Win.	Coke	Wod.
Drosier Edward, farmer, West Rudham			
Howard Thomas, ditto, ditto			
Winn Robert, shepherd, ditto	6	7	3

Runcton North.

	Win.	Coke	Wod.
Bayfield Joseph, farmer, North Runcton			
Cooper Thomas, ditto, ditto			
Gales Thomas, gent. ditto			
Jessup Robert, yeoman, ditto			
Morris Jeremiah, farmer, Garveston			
Merrison Jonathan, gent. North Runcton			
Oldmeadow Thomas, ditto, ditto	3	3	0

Runham.

	Win.	Coke	Wod.
Bayes John, labourer, Runham			
Burrow Samuel, gardener, ditto			
Dean Thomas, husbandman, ditto			
Fish Richard, farmer, Yarmouth			
Knights Edward, husbandman, Runham			
Lincoln James, farmer, ditto			
London R. M. husbandman, ditto	2	4	4

Runham.

	Win.	Coke	Wod.
Palmer Edmund, farmer, Filby			
Smith Benjamin, ditto, Runham			
Ward Samuel, husbandman, Acle	8	8	2

Runhall.

	Win.	Coke	Wod.
Hawkes John, farmer, Runhall			
Palmer John, ditto, ditto			
Thurling Peter, ditto, ditto	1	1	2

Runton.—North Erpingham Hund.

	Win.	Coke	Wod.
Abbs John, yeoman, Runton			
Abbs Francis, cordwainer, ditto			
Adcock John, carrier, ditto			
Carr John, jun. yeoman, ditto			
Fuller Webb John, cordwainer, ditto			
Johnson Paul, clerk, ditto			
Nave William, yeoman, ditto			
Pank Francis, ditto, ditto	8	8	0

Rushall.

	Win.	Coke	Wod.
Brighton James, farmer, Rushall			
Buskard William, ditto, ditto			
Meen Richard, ditto, ditto			
Mullenger James, ditto, ditto			
Prime William, ditto, ditto			
Smith Thomas, ditto, ditto	3	4	3

Rushford with Shadwell.

	Win.	Coke	Wod.
Buxton Sir Robert, bart. Rushford	0	0	1

Ruston East.

	Win.	Coke	Wod.
Atkinson Thomas, farmer, East Ruston			
Barber Thomas, ditto, ditto			
Bean John, ditto, ditto			
Durrell Joseph, ditto, ditto			
Durrel Charles, ditto, ditto			
Flaxman Samuel, boatman, ditto			
Gaze Robert, farmer, ditto			
Humfrey Richard, yeoman, ditto			
Plummer Charles, ditto, ditto			
Postle Samuel, farmer, ditto			
Postle Augustine, ditto, ditto			

Ruston East.

	Win.	Coke	Wod.
Rudd John, gent. East Ruston			
Shingles John, farmer, Happisburgh	1	1	12

Ryburgh Great.

	Win.	Coke	Wod.
Bell Martin, blacksmith, Great Ryburgh			
Davy Richard, farmer, ditto			
Flavill Joseph W. clerk, Stody			
Fowell Thomas, miller, Ovington			
Francis John, farmer, Great Ryburgh			
Gotts Daniel, carpenter, ditto			
Harman Thomas, farmer, ditto			
Howes John, ditto, ditto	1	2	7

Ryburgh Little.

	Win.	Coke	Wod.
Purling William, farmer, Little Ryburgh			
Rust Robert, blacksmith, ditto	2	2	0

Saham Toney.

	Win.	Coke	Wod.
Bowgen Hugh, farmer, Saham Toney			
Brighton Robert, ditto, ditto			
Butolph Jn. school-master, Wramplingham			
Clarke Edward, farmer, Saham Toney			
Clayton Sir William, bart. ditto			
French John, weaver, ditto			
Feaks Thomas, carpenter, ditto			
Gunn Haines, blacksmith, ditto			
Hardy Isaac, farmer, ditto			
Hardy John, ditto, ditto			
Kiddle William, labourer, ditto			
Kiddle Robert, farmer, ditto			
Knoppet Robert, ditto, ditto			
Mott John Thruston, esq. Barningham Parva			
Margetson Robert, ditto, Wicklewood			
Neal William, farmer, Saham Toney			
Ward Thomas, cordwainer, New Buckenham			
Whalebelly Thomas, farmer, Saham Toney			
Willimott Bell, labourer, ditto	4	6	15

Sall.

	Win.	Coke	Wod.
Gladdon William, yeoman, Marsham			
Jodrell R. Paul, jun. esq. Sall			
Vout John, carpenter, ditto	1	2	2

Salthouse.

	Win.	Coke	Wod.
Barber Benjamin, farmer, Thurlton			
Bussey Robert, ditto, Salthouse			
Campling John, ditto, ditto			
Lynford William, wheelwright, ditto			
Parrock Edward, yeoman, ditto			
Risebrook John, farmer, ditto			
Story Thomas, ditto, Bixley			
Sutton John, butcher, Panxworth	5	7	3

Salthouse.

	Win.	Coke	Wod.
Corben Joseph, yeoman, Holt			
Cranefield John, husbandman, Salthouse			
Cubitt William, yeoman, ditto			
Lowne William, husbandman, ditto			
Parson John, yeoman, ditto			
Proudfoot John, farmer, Yarmouth			
Spence John, carpenter, Salthouse	2	1	6

Sandringham.

	Win.	Coke	Wod.
Henley Henry Hoste, esq. Sandringham	0	1	1

Santon.

	Win.	Coke	Wod.
Garner John, farmer, Thetford	1	1	0

Saxlingham Nethergate.

	Win.	Coke	Wod.
Bales Thomas, farmer, Field-dalling			
Capon Charles, ditto, Saxlingham Nethergate			
Chittock Joseph, ditto, ditto			
Cockerill Roger, ditto, ditto			
Gordon William, clerk, ditto			
Gooch Thomas, ditto, ditto			
Hurrell Thomas, farmer, Little Dunham			
Plummer Robert, gent. Saxlingham Nether.			
Redgrave Joseph, farmer, ditto			
Riseborough William, ditto, Field-dalling			
Wainford James, farmer, Saxlingham N.			
Watson George, ditto, ditto	8	9	4

Saxlingham Thorpe.

	Win.	Coke	Wod.
Oughton Steph. farmer, Saxlingham Thorpe	1	1	0

Saxthorpe.

	Win.	Coke	Wod.
Allen John, farmer, Bawdeswell			
Bacon William, yeoman, Saxthorpe			
Cubitt Robert, ditto, Thwaite			
Gay John Johnson, gent. Gunthorpe			
Hill Robert, yeoman, Saxthorpe			
Westney William, gent. ditto			
Wiggett William, farmer, Edgefield			
Witherel Thomas, yeoman, Saxthorpe	5	6	3

Scarning.

	Win.	Coke	Wod.
Bates Samuel, farmer, Yaxham			
Bone John, ditto, Scarning			
Clarke William, ditto, ditto			
Girling Christ. esq. ditto			
Goddard Robert, farmer, Shipdham			
Hart George, ditto, Scarning			
Johnson ———, D. D. Yaxham			
Moore Francis, smith, Wendling			
Neave John, farmer, Great Fransham			
Priest St. John, clerk, Reepham			
Redgment Robert, farmer, Diss			
Riches William, ditto, Scarning			
Shilling William, ditto, Sporle	10	12	4

Scole or Osmodeston.

	Win.	Coke	Wod.
Balls Hezek. carpenter, Scole			
Debbenham Thomas, hosier, Scole			
Dove John, clerk, ditto			
Drane William, farmer, ditto			
Gooderham James, ditto, ditto			
Minns Thomas, ditto, ditto			
Pettet John, ditto, ditto			
Pitts John, linen-draper, New Buckenham			
Rodwell John, blacksmith, Scole			
Smith George, farmer, Frenze			
Tye Charles, ditto, Bressingham	3	4	9

Scottow.

	Win.	Coke	Wod.
Brown William, yeoman, Scottow			
Cadge William, miller, Sloley	0	0	2

Sharrington.

Cork John, yeoman, Sharington
Constable John, ditto, ditto
Girdlestone Robert, ditto, ditto
Tyrner John, carpenter, ditto

Win.	Coke	Pod.
4	3	0

Shelfanger.

Dodd Charles, farmer, Shelfanger
Dodd William, ditto, ditto
Ellis Henry, ditto, Tibbenham
Ellis Richard, ditto, Shelfanger
Freeman Charles, ditto, ditto
Hubbard Richard, labourer, ditto
Self John, carpenter, ditto
Wallis Seth, blacksmith, ditto
Wiseman David, farmer, ditto

Win.	Coke	Pod.
6	6	3

Shelton.

Drake Thomas, clerk, Intwood
Farrow William, farmer, Barnham Broome
Ward James, ditto, Shelton
Ward Edward, ditto, ditto

Win.	Coke	Pod.
2	2	3

Shereford.

Coney Thomas, farmer, Scuthorpe

Win.	Coke	Pod.
0	1	0

Sherringhams.

Barcham Benjamin, merchant, Sheringham
Chamberlin Corba, yeoman, ditto
Cook Flower, esq. ditto
Cranefield Wm. land-surveyor, Baconsthorpe
Cranefield Corba, ditto, Sheringham
Cubitt Robert, yeoman, ditto
Harrison Gregory, surveyor, Yarmouth
Hewett John Short, clerk, Southrepps
Matthews William, labourer, Sheringham
Pegg Thomas, yeoman, ditto
Pegg Henry, ditto, ditto
Pegg John, ditto, ditto
Wilson John, fisherman, ditto

Win.	Coke	Pod.
9	8	5

Shimpling.

Blake Philip, farmer, Shimpling
Calver Henry, ditto, Diss

Scoulton.

Hardy John, farmer, Hingham
Mason Robert, ditto, Cranworth

Win.	Coke	Wod.
1	1	1

Scratby.

Green John, husbandman, Scratby
Woolstone Benjamin, ditto, ditto
Woolston Robert, farmer, ditto

Win.	Coke	Wod.
5	3	0

Sculthorpe.

Jones Matthew, clerk, Sculthorpe
Kindle Joseph, blacksmith, ditto
Price William, farmer, ditto
Rayner Benjamin, ditto, ditto
Simmons Edward, labourer, ditto

Win.	Coke	Wod.
5	5	0

Sedgeford.

Clowes Edward, farmer, Halvergate
Forster John, ditto, Sedgeford
Lake William, ditto, ditto
Potter John, ditto, ditto
Read Thomas, ditto, Horningtoft
Rolfe Edmund, jun. esq. Sedgeford
Sampson M. A. farmer, Holme next the Sea
Sampson Augustus, ditto, ditto
Weatherhead Thomas, clerk, Sedgeford
Yaxley James, smith, Heacham

Win.	Coke	Wod.
10	9	0

Seething.

Chasteney William, gardener, Seething
Crickmore William, farmer, ditto
Grimmer Robert, ditto, ditto
Harvey Richard, wheelwright, Hempnall
Harvey Thomas, carpenter, Seething
Kett Thomas, esq. ditto
Kett George Samuel, esq. Bergh Apton
Smith William, farmer, Seething

Win.	Coke	Wod.
3	4	5

Setchy.

Foy Edmund, tanner, King's Lynn
Panton John, farmer, Setchy
Pridgeon Samuel, innholder, Tottenhill
Roper John, ditto, Setchy

Win.	Coke	Wod.
4	4	0

Win.	Coke	Wod,

Shimpling.

Chaplin William, labourer, Shimpling
Cooper James, farmer, ditto
Etheridge William, ditto, ditto
Felgate John, steward, Dickleburgh
Harrison Henry, clerk, Shimpling

Shipdham.

Andrews Wm. farmer, East Dereham
Alcock William, farmer, Shipdham
Bagg John, carpenter, ditto
Blomfield James, ditto, ditto
Booker Thomas, tanner, ditto
Butcher William, bricklayer, ditto
Barrett Charles D. surgeon, ditto
Bullock Colby, clerk, ditto
Catton John, baker, ditto
Clements John, miller, ditto
Coe Robert, farmer, East Bradenham
Coker Fuller, bricklayer, Shipdham
Coker William, gent. ditto
Dunnett Daniel, blacksmith, ditto
Farrow William, gent. ditto
Fuller Thomas, maltster, ditto
Gibson William, farmer, Westfield
Green John, ditto, Shipdham
Hall Thomas, ditto, ditto
Harvey James, ditto, ditto
Kitmer Thomas, tailor, ditto
Large William, baker, ditto
L'Edridge Charles, clerk, ditto
Oldfield Robert, wheelwright, ditto
Peck William, farmer, ditto
Platfoot Robert, tailor, Scarning
Redhead William, farmer, Forncet St. M.
Rust Stephen, ditto, Carbrooke
Savage John, ditto, Swaffham
Stagg James, cordwainer, Shipdham
Task Henry, farmer, ditto
Thurrell Richard, ironmonger, Necton
Vaper Thomas, gent. Shipdham
White Timothy, farmer, ditto
Whitret William, ditto, ditto

Win.	Coke	Wod,
6	6	1
4	11	33

Win.	Coke	Wod

Shotesham All Saints.

Aldred Thos. bricklayer, Shotesham All Saints
Bunn Charles, farmer, Hempnall
Dady David, weaver, Shotesham All Saints
Howlett John, gardener, Yarmouth
Ringer William, farmer, Forncet St. Peter
Scales Wm. carpenter, Shotesham All Saints

Win.	Coke	Wod
5	5	1

Shotesham St. Mary.

Boyce Francis, glazier, Shotesham St. Mary
Calthorpe John, gent, ditto
Fellowes Robert, esq. ditto
Spalding T. farmer, Saxlingham Nethergate

Win.	Coke	Wod
3	3	1

Shotesham St. Martin.

Notley Robert, farmer, Shotesham St. Martin

Win.	Coke	Wod
1	1	0

Shouldham.—Clackclose Hund.

Barkham Christopher, miller, Shouldham
Baxter John, yeoman, ditto
Browne Isaac, ditto, ditto
Batter William, farmer, ditto
Cooke William, ditto, ditto
Cozens Thomas, ditto, Marham
Holiman John, carpenter, Shouldham
Leech William, smith, Berston
Maltby Thomas, yeoman, Shouldham
Russell John, ditto, ditto
Scott Thomas, farmer, ditto

Win.	Coke	Wod
11	11	0

Shouldham Thorpe.

Browne Jacob, farmer, Shouldham Thorpe
Dickerson Robert, ditto, ditto
Easter William, ditto, ditto
Edwards John, ditto, ditto

Shropham.

Barrett Jonas, farmer, Shropham
Barrett John, higler, ditto
Calver Samuel, gent. Banham
Davey Robert, cordwainer, Attleborough
Harvey George, farmer, Shropham
Hetherset James, gent. ditto
Juby Edmund, farmer, Hempnall

Win.	Coke	Wod
4	4	0
7	7	0

	Win.	Coke	Wod.

Snettisham.

	Win.	Coke	Wod.
Grant George, esq. Snettisham			
Kitton Charles, farmer, Candley			
Lay James, grocer, Snettisham			
Lake Edmund, smith, ditto			
Pretty James, farmer, ditto			
Sadler Jeremiah, labourer, ditto			
Styleman Henry, esq. ditto			
Stanton Richard, gent. Darsingham	9	10	2

Snoring Great.

	Win.	Coke	Wod.
Bray William, farmer, Great Snoring			
Craske Thomas, ditto, Hindringham			
Fawcett James, clerk, Great Snoring			
Flemming John, esq. ditto			
Green Francis, farmer, Yaxham			
Leader William, ditto, Great Snoring			
Parnell Henry, ditto, ditto			
Ramm William, labourer, Kettlestone			
Rix William, farmer, Great Snoring			
Tuck William, sen. ditto, Little Snoring			
Wright James, gent. Great Snoring	7	10	5

Snoring Little.

	Win.	Coke	Wod.
Barnes Matthew, labourer, Little Snoring			
Gowers Marshall, ditto, ditto			
Laws Samuel, wool-comber, ditto			
Otley John, grocer, ditto			
Tuck William, carpenter, ditto			
Wright Samuel, farmer, ditto	5	4	1

Somerton East.

	Win.	Coke	Wod.
Dybatl Humphrey, husbandman, E. Somerton			
Huntington John Barker, gent. ditto.	0	0	2

Somerton West.

	Win.	Coke	Wod.
Crowe Thomas, farmer, Ormesby			
Hales William, ditto, West Somerton			
Jealous Thomas, ditto, ditto			
Manship William, ditto, Martham			
Rising William, ditto, ditto	0	0	5

	Win.	Coke	Wod.

Sisland.

	Win.	Coke	Wod.
Browne Joseph, gent. Tuttington			
Tibbenham Robert, farmer, Sisland	1	1	1

Skeyton.

	Win.	Coke	Wod.
Bidwell John, yeoman, Skeyton			
Bagden Thomas, ditto, ditto			
Cook William, ditto, ditto			
Jones Samuel, ditto, ditto			
Wortley John, ditto, ditto	3	4	2

Sloley.

	Win.	Coke	Wod.
Colman Edward, yeoman, Sloley			
Cubitt Benjamin, clerk, ditto			
Steward Samuel, wheelwright, ditto	0	0	3

Smallburgh.

	Win.	Coke	Wod.
Atlams Joseph, gent. Smallburgh			
Aufrere Philip Duval, clerk, Eccles			
Brundall Benjamin, cordwainer, Smallburgh			
Dix Richard, surgeon, ditto			
Gunn William, clerk, ditto			
Harvey John, farmer, ditto			
Marston Thomas, ditto, ditto			
Nave William, ditto, ditto			
Nave William, yeoman, ditto			
Postle John, gent. ditto			
Read John, farmer, Mattishall	3	5	8

Snarehill.

	Win.	Coke	Wod.
Redhead Thomas, esq. Snarehill	0	0	1

Snetterton.

	Win.	Coke	Wod.
Edwards Francis, cordwainer, Snetterton			
Fisk John, farmer, Starston			
Rudd Henry, ditto, Winfarthing			
Webster John, labourer, Snetterton	3	3	1

Snettisham.

	Win.	Coke	Wod.
Davis John, farmer, South Creek			
Egmore Richard, bricklayer, Docking			
Fayers John, farmer, Snettisham			

Southacre.

Clarke John, farmer, Wiggenhall St. Mary
Hogg Martin, clerk, Southacre
Seppings William, farmer, Clenchwarton

	Win.	Coke	Wod.
	1	3	2

Southbergh.

Daynes William, farmer, Hingham
Knowles Simon, husbandman, Southbergh
Starke Peter, farmer, Hingham
Starkey Robert, ditto, Southbergh

	Win.	Coke	Wod.
	0	3	4

Southery.

Bennett Philip, yeoman, Southery
Boycatt Thomas, miller, ditto
Burnham Edward, yeoman, Southery
Butcher Edmund, farmer, ditto
Constable William, yeoman, ditto
Galley John, farmer, ditto
Osler George, ditto, ditto
Peckett William, grocer, ditto
Peckett Robert, yeoman, ditto
Porter Thomas, farmer, ditto
Porter Samuel, yeoman, ditto
Porter Robert, farmer, ditto
Porter Christopher, ditto, ditto
Porter Christopher, yeoman, ditto
Porter Gregory, ditto, ditto
Porter John, ditto, ditto
Porter William, ditto, ditto
Proctor William, carpenter, ditto
Register William, farmer, ditto
Sayle Robert, ditto, ditto
Smith Thomas, ditto, ditto
Smith Samuel, ditto, ditto
Vipan Benjamin, ditto, Feltwell
Ward Henry, ditto, Southery
Ward John, ditto, ditto
Weasenham Thomas, ditto, ditto
Youles William, carpenter, ditto

	Win.	Coke	Wod.
	21	22	4

Southwood.

Anguish John, husbandman, Southwood
Tuthill Henry, farmer, Wickhampton

	Win.	Coke	Wod.
	2	2	0

Sparham.

Blomfield William, farmer, Carbrooke
Mason William, ditto, Sparham
Nelson James, ditto, Yaxham
Stoughton James, clerk, Sparham
Wells Thomas, shepherd, ditto

	Win.	Coke	Wod.
	5	5	0

Spixworth.

Longe Francis, esq. Spixworth

	Win.	Coke	Wod.
	0	0	1

Sporle with Palgrave.

Cozens Henry, carpenter, Sporle
Hodson Tillett, thatcher, ditto
Newton Casar, farmer, ditto
Pearson William, ditto, ditto
Smyth John, ditto, ditto

	Win.	Coke	Wod.
	2	3	3

Sprowston.

Cozens Jeremiah, farmer, Sprowston
Fox William, wheelwright, ditto
Hubbard John, yeoman, ditto
King James, farmer, ditto
King William, ditto, ditto
Kingsbury William, ditto, ditto
Rossigrol J. G. yeoman, ditto
Wilks Mark, farmer, ditto

Stalham.

Atkins Thomas, farmer, Stalham
Burney Joseph, clerk, Southrepps
Bubbins Martin, wheelwright, Salthouse
Burton Thomas, yeoman, Stalham
Burton Robert, schoolmaster, ditto
Cooke Robert, farmer, ditto
Cook Samuel, miller, ditto
Cubit Benjamin, farmer, ditto
Hindle Daniel, plumber, ditto
Johnson James, farmer, ditto
Lyon James, cabinet-maker, ditto
Pycraft Nathaniel, dealer, ditto
Sieley John, surgeon, ditto
Silcock Obadiah, shopkeeper, ditto
Ulph Robert, farmer, ditto
Withers Thomas, baker, ditto

	Win.	Coke	Wod.
	7	8	1
	7	6	12

126

	Win.	Coke	Wod.

Stanfield.

Bradfield Charles, farmer, Stanfield
Bradfield Charles, jun. ditto, ditto
Buck Henry, labourer, Tasburgh
Hutchin William, farmer, Stanfield
Quantrell William, ditto, Tasburgh
Smith William, ditto, Stanfield
Sooley John, ditto, ditto
Young Robert, ditto, Walsoken

6 6 2

Stanford.

Horne Robert, farmer, Thetford

0 0 1

Stanhoe.

Hare Frederick, esq. Stanhoe
Howard Edward, carpenter, ditto
Spooner William, wheelwright, ditto

3 3 0

Starston.

Burgess Robert, blacksmith, Starston
Cole William, farmer, Earsham
Cutting John, ditto, Starston
Fisk George, ditto, ditto
Hart Thomas, ditto, ditto
Howard Robert, ditto, ditto
Oldershaw John, clerk, Redenhall
Theobald John, farmer, Starston
Whitear William, clerk, ditto

3 6 6

Stibbard.

Bell Philip, aledraper, Stibbard
Frary Thomas, gent. ditto
Sharr John, farmer, ditto
Sharr Richard, ditto, ditto
Southgate Samuel, wheelwright, ditto
Wittrick John, yeoman, Woodnorton
Withers Peter, gent. Stibbard

5 6 2

Stifkey.

Buck James, farmer, Stifkey
Lambert John, gardener, ditto
Wightman Thomas, carrier, ditto

2 1 1

R

130

	Win.	Coke	Wod.

Stockton.

Bond Robert, esq. Stockton
Larke Robert, farmer, Gillingham All Saints
Turner Daniel, servant, Geldeston

0 0 3

Stody.

Paul Henry, farmer, Stody

0 0 1

Stoke Holy Cross.

Chapman John, farmer, Little Melton
Mann Edmund Scott, ditto, Stoke Holy Cross
Riches R. ditto, Morley St. Botolph

3 3 0

Stoke Ferry.

Blomfield James, butcher, Stoke Ferry
Bradfield James, gent. ditto
Curtis Richard, farmer, ditto
Etheridge Anthony, grocer, Thwaite
Flower John, victualler, Stoke
Green Thomas, miller, ditto
Hibgame William, maltster, ditto
Kidd John, carpenter, ditto
Micklefield Roger, gent. ditto
Morley Henry, ditto, Stoke Ferry
Powell John, shoe-maker, Stoke
Salmon Thomas, merchant, Stoke Ferry
Sanders Charles, farmer, ditto
West Abraham, grocer, ditto

4 7 10

Stokesby.

Daniel Richard, farmer, Stokesby
Miller John, blacksmith, ditto
Norton James, farmer, ditto

1 1 2

Stow Bardolph.

Bell Philip, clerk, Stow Bardolph
Bultitaft William, farmer, Wormegay
Hare Thomas, esq. Stow Bardolph
Hudson William, farmer, Wimbotsham
Ice John, ditto, Stow Bardolph
Roper Thomas, ditto, Wormegay
White George, carpenter, Stow Bardolph
Wignoll John, yeoman, ditto

7 8 0

Stow Bedon.

Elden Thomas, farmer, Hingham
Greengrass Thomas, labourer, Stow Bedon
Lunt Robert, farmer, Caston

	Win.	Coke	Wod.
Stow Bedon	0	1	3

Stradsett.

Harper Lawrence, farmer, Stow Bardolph

	Win.	Coke	Wod.
Stradsett	1	1	0

Stratton St. Mary.

Aldred James, jun. farmer, Stratton St. M.
Aldis James, schoolmaster, ditto
Alburgh John, butcher, ditto
Barnes Elisha, sen. peruke-maker, ditto
Bassingthwaite James, farmer, ditto
Bensly William, carpenter, ditto
Buroughes Ellis, clerk, ditto
Fryer John, farmer, ditto
Hearne James, cordwainer, ditto
Howes John, farmer, ditto
Hudson Richard, ditto, ditto
Land Jeremiah, ditto, ditto
Long James, ditto, Hardwick
Long Henry, tailor, Deopham
Swann Thomas, bricklayer, Saxlingham N.
Utting John, surgeon, Aslacton
Walford William, clerk, Stratton St. Mary

	Win.	Coke	Wod.
Stratton St. Mary	4	6	13

Stratton St. Michael.

Bloy Francis, farmer, Stratton St. Michael
D'Oyley William, clerk, ditto
Parkerson J. C. farmer, ditto

	Win.	Coke	Wod.
Stratton St. Michael	1	1	2

Stratton Strawless.

Marsham Robert, esq. Stratton Strawless
Savage John, yeoman, Hevingham

	Win.	Coke	Wod.
Stratton Strawless	0	0	2

Strumpshaw.

Atkins Thomas, farmer, Strumpshaw
Browne Thomas, gent. Beighton
Hylton William, blacksmith, Strumpshaw
Manning William, carpenter, ditto
Nelson William, clerk, ditto
Randall Paul, blacksmith, Palling

R 2

Strumpshaw.

Smith Edward, miller, Halvergate
Spooner R. D. R. clerk, Strumpshaw
Stannard William, farmer, ditto
Tuck Thomas, ditto, ditto
Wells Jonas, ditto, ditto
Withers John, bricklayer, Strumpshaw

	Win.	Coke	Wod.
Strumpshaw	6	6	6

Starston.

Leech Thomas, gent. Diss

	Win.	Coke	Wod.
Starston	1	1	0

Suffield.

Petre John, esq. Westwick

	Win.	Coke	Wod.
Suffield	0	0	1

Surlingham.

Barnes Edward, farmer, Surlingham
Bately John, ditto, ditto
Besfor Robert, boatwright, ditto
Creek Edward, blacksmith, ditto
Dawson Charles, husbandman, ditto
Garrod Thomas, labourer, ditto
Gent John, farmer, ditto
Murrell Thomas, husbandman, ditto
Rudd Joseph, farmer, ditto
Rudd John, ditto, ditto
Wegg Whaites, husbandman, Upton

	Win.	Coke	Wod.
Surlingham	5	6	6

Sustead.

Johnson John, yeoman, Overstrand
Tyrrell John, cordwainer, Sustead

	Win.	Coke	Wod.
Sustead	2	2	0

Sutton.

Armes David, yeoman, Sutton
Bane John, farmer, ditto
Barber Robert, ditto, ditto
Bray William, ditto, ditto
Bygrave John, ditto, ditto
Carr John, ditto, ditto
Clear John, publican, Acle
Crowe Robert, farmer, Sutton
Durrant Samuel, yeoman, ditto
Jinson Paul, ditto, ditto
Savory William, farmer, ditto

	Win.	Coke	Wod.
Sutton	1	6	7

Swaffham.

Name	Win.	Coke	Wod.
Bailey John Horatio, surgeon, Swaffham			
Barker William, linen-weaver, ditto			
Blomfield Francis, gent. Fersfield			
Blox Francis, sadler, Swaffham			
Clarke John Jacob, farmer, Beetley			
Crowe Philip, shopkeeper, ditto			
Dalton Francis, esq. Swaffham			
Dix Robert, sadler, ditto			
Dugmore John, esq. West Bradenham			
Finch Jacob, druggist, Swaffham			
Gage Michael, yeoman, Shouldham			
Horne Robert, baker, Stoke Ferry			
Kiddle Robert, ditto, Swaffham			
Lancaster John, blacksmith, ditto			
Ling Stephen, bricklayer, ditto			
Lockwood Benjamin, watch-maker, ditto			
Mason John, gent. Whinbergh			
Martin Henry, ditto, Castleacre			
Page James, brewer, Swaffham			
Parsons James, labourer, ditto			
Plowright George, farmer, East Dereham			
Plowright John, cooper, ditto			
Powley William, bricklayer, Swaffham			
Pymar William, farmer, ditto			
Pymar William, jun. ditto, Holme Hale			
Rix William, farmer, Swaffham			
Rust John, innkeeper, ditto			
Say Henry, clerk, ditto			
Sharpen Edward, clerk, ditto			
Stratton John, farmer, ditto			
Stuckey William, jun. ditto, Northwold			
Wilbraham Roger, esq. Little Fransham			
Woor Thomas William, waiter, Yarmouth			
Wright John, farmer, Marlingford			
Wright Francis, miller, Swaffham			
Yonge William, clerk, Swaffham			
Young Henry, watch-maker, Castleacre			

Swafield.

Name	Win.	Coke	Wod.
Kemp J. B. farmer, North Walsham			
Scott George, gent. Gimmingham	18	25	22
	1	1	1

Swainsthorpe.

Name	Win	Coke	Wod.
Branford Richard, innkeeper, Saxlingham			
Mayes William Freezer, farmer, Swainsthorpe	0	0	2

Swannington.

Name	Win	Coke	Wod.
Allen Thomas, yeoman, Swannington			
Dewing Zachariah, ditto, ditto			
Howlett Benjamin, shoe-maker, ditto			
Howlett Bryant, farmer, Alderford			
Howlett James, ditto, Swannington			
Leath John, yeoman, ditto			
Lowe Samuel, farmer, ditto			
Neal Barnard, yeoman, ditto			
Pye John, farmer, Felthorpe			
Rous John, carpenter, Swannington			
Vickers John, clerk, ditto	3	4	8

Swanton Abbots.

Name	Win	Coke	Wod.
Bartram Robert, yeoman, Swanton Abbots			
Blake William, esq. ditto			
Cooper Daniel, labourer, ditto			
Cook William, gent. Lammas			
Ducker Daniel, yeoman, Swanton Abbots	2	3	3

Swanton Morley.

Name	Win	Coke	Wod.
Barber Samuel, farmer, Swanton Morley			
Baker William, ditto, ditto			
Collett William, clerk, Surlingham			
Emms Samuel, sen. farmer, East Bilney			
Emms Samuel, ditto, Swanton Morley			
Freeman John, ditto, Kimberley			
Mack Thomas, farmer, Elsing			
Mays John, butcher, Swanton Morley			
Rix Peter, farmer, ditto			
Spencer John, ditto, ditto			

Swanton Novers.

Name	Win	Coke	Wod.
Cossey Thomas, carpenter, Swanton Novers			
Dew Richard, yeoman, Brinningham			
Dew John, farmer, Swanton Novers			
Emerson John, carpenter, Hindolveston			
Fox John, pelter, Swanton Novers			
Giles Samuel, labourer, ditto	7	8	3

Swanton Novers.

Win. Coke Wod.

Kendle Charles, gent. Holt
Laws Simon, wool-comber, Swanton Novers
Moore William, ditto, ditto
Rix Thomas, farmer, ditto
Wells Robert, ditto, Felmingham — 10 | 10 | 1

Swardeston.

Browne Peter, bricklayer, Swardeston
Buck James, carpenter, Wreningham
Cannell Francis, gardener, Swardeston
Jeffries Robert, farmer, ditto
Kemp James, ditto, ditto
Smith William, ditto, East Carlton — 0 | 1 | 6

Syderstone.

Kingston George, clerk, Syderstone
Savory John, farmer, Bintry — 2 | 1 | 0

Syderstrand.

Amis William, yeoman, Syderstrand
Blyth William, ditto, ditto
Flaxman James, gent. ditto
Nurse James, ditto, Trimmingham
Warnes James, miller, Syderstrond
Wordley Robert, yeoman, Southrepps — 6 | 4 | 2

Tacolneston.

Arnold John, Bunwell
Beverley Samuel, farmer, Saxlingham Net.
Blomfield James, ditto, Tacolneston
Browne Archer, ditto, ditto
Browne John, esq. Morley St. Peter
Fox Robert, farmer, Tacolneston
Howes James, ditto, Fundenhall
Warren John, clerk, Tacolneston — 1 | 1 | 6

Tasburgh.

Broadbank Thomas, gent. Tasburgh
Clarke Somers, farmer, ditto
Goward Matthias, gent. ditto
Millett William, farmer, Framingham Pigot
Stannard Philip, clerk, Tasburgh — 4 | 4 | 1

Tatterford.

Win. Coke Wot.

Dorr John, farmer, Hindringham
Norris Robert, clerk, Tivetshall — 0 | 1 | 2

Taverham.

Branthwayt M. S. esq. Taverham
Bunnett James, farmer, Ringland
Culley Henry, ditto, Ashby
Hewett William, ditto, East Dereham
Mouse John, carpenter, Yarmouth — 5 | 5 | 0

Terrington St. Clement.

Bentinck Wm. admiral, Terrington St. Cl.
Bunting William, farmer, ditto
Carter William, ditto, ditto
Fisher William, ditto, ditto
Fisher Michael, ditto, ditto
Goode Ambrose, clerk, ditto
Reader George, ditto, ditto
Skiell Robert, ditto, ditto
Smith John, ditto, ditto
Stevenson Abner, ditto, ditto
Wright Robert, ditto, ditto
Wright William, ditto, ditto
Wright James, ditto, ditto

Terrington St. John.

Bell William, surgeon, Terrington St. John
Burrell James, farmer, ditto
Eggleton John, ditto, ditto
Johnson Thomas, ditto, ditto
Mann James, publican, ditto
Sutterby Henry, jun. farmer, ditto
Sutterby James, sen. ditto ditto
Sutterby Robert, ditto, Tilney St. Lawrence
Sutterby H. sen. ditto, Terrington St. John
Sutterby William, ditto, ditto
Tyson John, clerk, King's Lynn
Wright John, farmer, Terrington St. John
Wright Gregory, ditto, ditto — 12 | 12 | 1

Tharston.

Beckett James, farmer, Tharston
Browne Robert, ditto, ditto — 7 | 7 | 7

Tharston.

Burcham Thomas, farmer, Tharston
Hart Thomas, ditto, ditto
Mere Robert, labourer, ditto
Parslee Joseph, farmer, ditto
Rix George, husbandman, ditto
Stannard Benjamin, farmer, Wacton
Thurston Robert, ditto, Tharston
Wicks Robert, ditto, ditto

Thelverton or Thelton.

Clarke Thomas, farmer, Thelverton
Musket John, ditto, Tasburgh

Themilthorpe.

Hendry James, yeoman, Foxley

Thetford.

Adams John, cordwainer, Thetford
Arbon James, bricklayer, ditto
Austin Thomas, labourer, ditto
Baker Noah, auctioneer, ditto
Baker William Wisson, auctioneer, ditto
Bartlett Robert, ———, ditto
Bartlett Gordon, gent. Great Cressingham
Barnes John, millwright, Thetford
Baldrick Edmund, cordwainer, ditto
Bidford Leonard Shelford, esq. ditto
Bidwell Shelford, esq. ditto
Boldero George, clerk, Kilverstone
Boyce James, butcher, Thetford
Burrell Joseph, ironfounder, ditto
Churchyard John, cordwainer, ditto
Chapman Benjamin, gent. ditto
Clarke William, labourer, ditto
Clarke William Culyer, leather-cutter, ditto
Claxon Edmund, paper-maker, ditto
Clements John, labourer, ditto
Coates William, carpenter, ditto
Davey George, victualler, ditto
Dent William, ditto, ditto
Dugmore Thomas, gent. Downham
Ellis John, tailor, Thetford

Thetford.

Faux John Burrell, draper, Thetford
Fitic James, nurseryman, ditto
Gates John, cordwainer, ditto
Galway Stephen Payne, esq. ditto
Gill Thomas Withers, merchant, ditto
Gissing Stephen, maltster, ditto
Gill Joseph. esq. ditto
Graham Fitt, shopkeeper, ditto
Hardy William, tanner, ditto
Hancock John, baker, ditto
Hewitt Thomas, carpenter, Northwold
Hill John, ditto, Thetford
Hollingworth William, miller, ditto
Harrold Philip, carpenter, ditto
Howard William, blacksmith, ditto
Hubbard William, carpenter, ditto
Hubbard Thomas, gardener, ditto
Inman Francis, carpenter, ditto
Juler John, grocer, ditto
Knowles Daniel, bricklayer
Linkhorn Storkard, labourer, ditto
Malt William, cordwainer, ditto
Manning Harry Charles, clerk, ditto
Marshall Griffin Wharf, cordwainer, ditto
Messling Thomas, victualler, ditto
Millard Edward, labourer, ditto
Mingay William Robert, M. D. ditto
Newbury George, gardener, ditto
Newman William, baker, ditto
Newell William, brickmaker, ditto
Oldman William, miller, ditto
Pawson Richard, paper-maker, ditto
Pratt Thomas, yeoman, ditto
Pratt John, victualler, ditto
Prick William, gent. ditto
Proctor George Beauchamp, esq. ditto
Palmer Edward, farmer, North Lopham
Pallant Robert, farrier, Thetford
Preston Henry, labourer, ditto
Purr James, gent. ditto
Rogers William, carpenter, ditto
Rogers Robert, wool-comber, Hockwold

Thetford.

Name	Win.	Coke	Wod.
Rolfe William, shopkeeper, Thetford			
Ross Morgan, surgeon, ditto			
Roberts Henry, maltster, ditto			
Rolfe John, carpenter, ditto			
Russell Edward, blacksmith, ditto			
Simmons John, currier, ditto			
Spinks Charles, labourer, ditto			
Spendlove John, watch-maker, ditto			
Sterne John, baker, ditto			
Sterne William, ditto, Methwold			
Stone John, carrier, Thetford			
Sterne John, hosier, ditto			
Sterne Salmon, cooper, ditto			
Sterne Thomas, carpenter, ditto			
Sewell Daniel, gent. Shouldham			
Slipper Thomas, baker, Thetford			
Stevens John, paper-maker, ditto			
Sterne Robert, carpenter, ditto			
Sterne Peter, cordwainer, ditto			
Sterne William, ditto, ditto			
Thompson Henry, gent. ditto			
Tuddenham Robert, jun. cooper, ditto			
Vipan Thomas, brewer, ditto			
Ward John, farmer, ditto	45	54	55
Watson Royall, aledraper, Northwold			
Willett Ingle, banker, Thetford			
Winterburn John, carpenter, ditto			
Whistler John, hair-dresser, ditto			
Wollard John, labourer, ditto			
Woods Charles, brewer, Attleborough	3	1	1

Thompson.

Name	Win.	Coke	Wod.
Bates Robert, farmer, Horningtoft			
Buckenham William, cordwainer, Thompson			
Harwood William Tooke, lieut. colonel, ditto			
Shuiver James, farmer, Carbrooke			

Thornage.

Name	Win.	Coke	Wod.
Abraham Robert, labourer, Bale			
Cook William, miller, Thornage			
Greeve John, carpenter, Letheringset			
Kendle James, farmer, Thornage			

s 2

Thornage.

Name	Win.	Coke	Wod.
Mann Francis, blacksmith, Sharrington			
Starling Richard, yeoman, Thornage			
Temple Thomas, farmer, Bunwell			
Williams William, gent. Thornage			
Wilcocks Wm. Wright, clk. Swanton Mor.	9	9	0

Thornham.

Name	Win.	Coke	Wod.
Bunton Thomas, butcher, Thornham			
Corston Robert, fisherman, ditto			
Hall William, carpenter, ditto			
Ivy John, farmer, ditto			
Rose William, carpenter, ditto	5	5	0

Thorpe, next Hadiscoe.—Claver. Hun.

Name	Win.	Coke	Wod.
Ames Daniel, gent. Stoke Holy Cross			
Last Samuel, farmer, Thurlton			
Last John, ditto, Thorpe	1	1	2

Thorpe Abbots.

Name	Win.	Coke	Wod.
Buckenham Thomas, farmer, Thorpe Abbot			
Knights Henry, ditto, Brockdish			
Knights Richard, ditto, Thorpe Abbots	2	2	1

Thorpe, next Norwich.

Name	Win.	Coke	Wod.
Basey Edmund, footman, Costessey			
Batley Thomas, farmer, Thorpe			
Borton John Drew, clerk, Blofield			
Harvey John, esq. Thorpe			
Humfrey Richard, clerk, ditto			
James Rice, esq. ditto			
Jessup John, labourer. ditto			
Massey Thomas, ironmonger, ditto			
Rainer John, gardener, ditto			
Robinson John, gent. ditto			
Suffield Henry, farmer, Salhouse			
Weston Charles, esq. Mattishall Bergh			
West Francis, gent. Thorpe			
Weeds John, carpenter, ditto			
Windett James, farmer, ditto	11	12	4

Thorpe Market.

Name	Win.	Coke	Wod.
Caston David, yeoman, Southrepps			
Martins John, gardener, Wood dalling	0	0	2

	Win.	Coke	Wod.
Threxton.			
Barton Thomas, gent. Threxton	0	0	1
Thrigby.			
Browne Thomas, farmer, Billockby	1	1	0
Thurgarton.			
Roger William, yeoman, Thurgarton			
Sayer Samuel, ditto, ditto			
Spurrell William, gent. ditto			
Spurrell William, yeoman, Bassingham			
Spurrell William, ditto, Aldborough	5	4	0
Thurlton.			
Barber William, sawyer, Thurlton			
Curtis James, blacksmith, ditto			
Disney James, miller, Norton Subcorse			
Garwood John, farmer, Thurlton			
Goodrich Richard, labourer, ditto			
Hunt John, farmer, ditto			
Minns David, schoolmaster, Shotesham			
Mool John, husbandman, Thurlton			
Pooley John, husbandman, ditto			
Pope Henry, thatcher, ditto			
Rushmer William, labourer, ditto			
Sayer Thomas, farmer, ditto			
Self John, husbandman, ditto			
Shardelow Samuel, cordwainer, ditto			
West Benjamin, carpenter, ditto	10	8	7
Thurne.			
Parker John, farmer, Thurne	0	0	1
Thurning.			
Davies Philip, farmer, Thurning			
Harris J. ditto, Fulmodeston			
Johnson Samuel, ditto, Thurning			
Powell Philip, gent. ditto	3	3	1
Thursford.			
Allen Robert, cordwainer, Hindringham			
Bloom Edward, farmer, Great Snoring			
Callow James, farmer, Thursford			
Leeder Benjamin, ditto, North Elmham	2	3	2

	Win.	Coke	Wod.
Thurton.			
Berry Daniel, farmer, Ashby			
Browne Robert, ditto, Surlingham			
Carver James, cordwainer, Thurton			
Utting William, gent. Moulton			
Utting Arthur, R. N. Thurton	2	3	3
Thurton.			
Palmer William, farmer, Thuxton			
Reynolds Daniel, husbandman, ditto			
Taylor John, farmer, Attleburgh			
Wortley Robert, ditto, Thuxton	3	3	1
Thwaite.—Loddon Hundred.			
Beckett Robert, husbandman, Woodton			
Gentleman George, ditto, Thwaite	1	1	1
Thwaite.—South Erpingham.			
Cook John, yeoman, Thwaite			
Woolsey John, ditto, ditto	2	2	0
Tibbenham.			
Betts Richard, butcher, Moulton			
Beverley Michael, farmer, Tibbenham			
Chasteney Philip, farmer, Forncet St. Peter			
Daynes Isaac, ditto, Tibbenham			
Goodrum William, ditto, ditto			
Reynolds John, ditto, ditto			
Rowing Archibald, ditto, ditto			
Rose William, ditto, ditto			
Snelling John, ditto, ditto			
Warren Thomas, ditto, ditto	2	5	8
Tilney All Saints.			
Baxter George, miller, Tilney All Saints			
Becket Wm. farmer, Wig. St. Mary Mag.			
Colt Thomas, cordwainer, Tilney All Saints			
Fisher Robert, farmer, ditto			
Parke Benjamin, clerk, ditto			
Scarnell John, blacksmith, ditto			
Snoxdell Oliver, farmer, ditto	4	4	3

Tilney St. Lawrence.

	Win.	Coke	Wod.
Browne William, publican, Tilney St. Law.			
Crown Edmund, farmer, ditto			
Hall William, ditto, ditto			
Hallowell John, ditto, ditto			
Lowden Austin, ditto, ditto			
Newman John, ditto, ditto			
Pollyn William, ditto, Walpole St. Peter			
Pollyn John, labourer, Tilney St. Lawrence			
Rockley John, farmer, ditto			
Scait John, ditto, ditto			
Scarnell William, ditto, ditto			
Sutterby Thomas, ditto, ditto			
Thimbleby Joseph, ditto, ditto			

Tilney cum Islington.

	Win.	Coke	Wod.
Coe Robert, farmer, Tilney cum Islington	8	7	5
Mills Alan, publican, Tilney St. Lawrence	2	2	0

Titchwell.

	Win.	Coke	Wod.
Browning Frederick, clerk, Titchwell	2	2	1
Emerson Isaac, gent. ditto			
Overton Clement, ditto, ditto			

Tittleshall.

	Win.	Coke	Wod.
Balls John, husbandman, Tittleshall			
Butler George, miller, ditto			
Forby William, gent. ditto			
Franklin William, farmer, ditto			
Hilling John, ditto, Beeston			
Lawson Jeremiah, ditto, Tittleshall			
Leeds Thomas, ditto, ditto			
Nichols William, bricklayer, ditto			
Riches Thomas, farmer, ditto			
Rix John, ditto, ditto			
Vincent William, butcher, ditto			
Wright Robert, blacksmith, ditto	12	12	0

Tivetshall.

	Win.	Coke	Wod.
Bell Benjamin, tanner, Tivetshall			
Coleby Caleb, linen-weaver, Tivetshall St. M.			
Gardiner Richard, gent. Tivetshall			
Gowing George, farmer, Moulton			

Tivetshall.

	Win.	Coke	Wod.
Gowing Thos. farmer, Tivetshall St.Margaret			
Hern Francis, ditto, Tivetshall			
Holmes John, ditto, ditto			
Self Robert, ditto, Besthorpe			
Shipley Richard, ditto, Tivetshall			
Snelling Joseph, ditto, ditto			
Snelling Joseph, ditto, Tivetshall St. Mary			
Spinks James, ditto, ditto			
Youngman Thomas, ditto, Bunwell	12	12	1

Tofts West.

	Win.	Coke	Wod.
Moseley John, esq. West Tofts	1	1	0

Toft Monks.

	Win.	Coke	Wod.
Carpenter William, gent. Toft Monks			
Denny Daniel, farmer, Norton			
Grimmer William, ditto, Toft Monks			
Hayward William, ditto, Garboldisham			
Last John, jun. ditto, Toft Monks			
Pleasants William, blacksmith, ditto	0	0	6

Toftrees.

	Win.	Coke	Wod.
Bale Edward, farmer, Fakenham			
Case Charles, ditto, Sculthorpe	1	2	1

Topcroft.

	Win.	Coke	Wod.
Beckett John, carpenter, Topcroft			
Borrett Henry, ditto, ditto			
Bunn John, farmer, Hempnall			
Delf William, ditto, Topcroft			
Jex John, ditto, Hempnall			
Richards James, jun. ditto, ditto			
Rounce Samuel, ditto, Topcroft			
Svanods John, woodman, ditto			
Wilson John, farmer, Hempnall	1	0	9

Tottenhill.

	Win.	Coke	Wod.
Cross William, farmer, Tottenhill			
Graves Benjamin, ditto, ditto			
Neale Rutledge, ditto, ditto			
Watkinson Francis, schoolmaster, Wereham.	3	3	1

Tottington.

Name	Win.	Coke	Wod.
Allen James, labourer, Tottington			
Burrows Robert, farmer, ditto			
Finch John, yeoman, ditto			
Neale John, ditto, ditto	0	0	4

Trimmingham.

Name	Win.	Coke	Wod.
Bacon William, yeoman, Erpingham			
Clipperton Robert, ditto, Trimmingham			
Clipperton Jonathan, ditto, ditto			
Gidney John, labourer, ditto			
Gilman Stephen, yeoman, Gimmingham			
Long Daniel, fisherman, Trimmingham			
Metcalf William, labourer, ditto			
Newman Joseph, yeoman, ditto			
Nurse Thomas, gent. ditto			
Plumley Richard, miller, ditto			
Royal John, yeoman, Beckham West	6	3	8

Trowse Newton.

Name	Win.	Coke	Wod.
Adair William, esq. Trowse Newton			
Browne John, farmer, ditto			
Cooke James, ditto, Thorpe			
Garrard John, ditto, Trowse Newton			
Money J. general, ditto	5	5	0

Trunch.

Name	Win.	Coke	Wod.
Amis John, yeoman, Trunch			
Bacon Richard, shopkeeper, ditto			
Frary William Oxley, gent. Knapton			
Howes William, yeoman, Trunch			
Lacey John, schoolmaster, ditto			
Long Robert, yeoman, ditto			
Primrose William, merchant, ditto			
Ward Marmaduke, clerk, ditto			
Wortley Samuel, ——— ditto	3	2	7

Tuddenham East.

Name	Win.	Coke	Wod.
Beeston Robert, farmer, Great Witchingham			
Garrard John, ditto, Kirby Bedon			
Gillett Robert, ditto, East Tuddenham			
Gooch John, ditto, ditto			
High Charles, ditto, ditto			

T

Tuddenham East.

Name	Win.	Coke	Wod.
Leech Robert, farmer, East Tuddenham			
Mellish Charles, clerk, ditto			
Sandall Richard, gent. Welborne			
Tunney John, farmer, East Tuddenham			
Tunney John, ditto, ditto			
Vasser William, ditto, ditto			
Webster Francis, gent. ditto	3	4	9

Tuddenham North.

Name	Win.	Coke	Wod.
Buscall Matthew, farmer, Wiveton			
Evans Thomas Browne, esq. N. Tuddenham			
Fitt Francis, farmer, ditto			
King Elling, blacksmith, ditto			
Mack Edward, farmer, ditto			
Shelford Leonard, clerk, ditto			
Springall William, farmer, Rockland			
Sussens William, ditto, North Tuddenham	6	6	2

Tunstall.

Name	Win.	Coke	Wod.
Batley Stephen, farmer, Tunstall			
Williams John, ditto, ditto	1	2	1

Tunstead.

Name	Win.	Coke	Wod.
Amis Joseph, farmer, Tunstead			
Bembridge Robert, carpenter, Sloley			
Foreman Andrew, yeoman, Tunstead			
Gales Henry, ditto, Sloley			
Hacon Dennis, farmer, Lingwood			
Mack Thomas, gent. Tunstead			
Mack Thomas, jun. ditto, ditto			
Parsons James, farmer, ditto			
Perkins Richard, ditto, ditto			
Scottow Thomas, yeoman, Ingham			
Shepherd John, sen. gent. Bacton			
Suffling Richard. thatcher, Sloley	1	1	11

Twyford.

Name	Win.	Coke	Wod.
Savory S. H. clerk, Bintry			
Savory Edward, farmer, ditto			
Savory Coulsey, ditto, Colkirk	0	0	3

Upton.

	Win.	Coke	Wod.
Browne James, bricklayer, Upton		—	—
Cater William, husbandman, ditto			—
Carson John, farmer, ditto		—	—
Davy John, husbandman, ditto			—
Day Jacob, farmer, ditto			—
Dawson Thomas, ditto, ditto			—
Day Thomas, ditto, ditto	—	—	
Diamond Thomas, ditto, ditto	—	—	
Docking Isaac, ditto, ditto			—
Francis William, husbandman, ditto			—
George Thomas, farmer, ditto			—
Harrison Edmund, butcher, South Walsham			—
Holmes John, farmer, Upton			—
Maddell William, ditto, ditto			—
Minister Edward, ditto, Wickhampton	—	—	
Smith Robert, blacksmith, Upton			—
Stout Simon, ~~ditto~~, ditto		—	—
Tungate Robert, carpenter, ditto			—
Tungate John, ditto, ditto			—
Waters William, farmer, ditto			—
Whaites Edward, ditto, Acle			—
	3	6	18

Upwell.—Freebridge Hundred.

	Win.	Coke	Wod.
Abraham William, cooper, Upwell			—
Berry Samuel, farmer, ditto			—
Burton Mark, yeoman, ditto			—
Chamberlin Thomas, carpenter, ditto	—		—
Climenson Joseph, farmer, Welney	—	—	
Coward William, ditto, Upwell			—
Darby Thomas, carpenter, ditto	—		—
Drake Robert, aledraper, Feltwell			—
Drake Thomas, yeoman, Upwell	—		—
Dunston William, farmer, ditto			—
Elmer William, ditto, ditto		—	—
Egar John, grocer, ditto		—	—
Eldred Daniel, farmer, ditto			—
Fearing Noah, ditto, ditto	—	—	
Facles James, ditto, ditto			—
Grimmer Robert, ditto, ditto			—
Goulding Thomas, schoolmaster, ditto			—
Hobourn William, farmer, ditto			—
Hodson Emanuel, ditto, ditto			—

Upwell.---Freebridge Hundred.

	Win.	Coke	Wod.
Hodson John, farmer, Welney			—
Hopkin William, ditto, Upwell			—
Kimmans Robert, ditto, ditto			—
Large William, ditto, ditto		—	—
Lee James, gent. ditto			—
Lee James, jun. grocer, Hilgay			—
Lemon Thomas, farmer, Upwell			—
Lee William, gent. Outwell			—
Lister Thomas, farmer, Upwell	—		—
Lister Henry, ditto, ditto			—
Long James, ditto, ditto	—	—	
Marshall Joseph, ditto, ditto	—	—	
Marshall John, ditto, ditto	—	—	
May John, ditto, ditto	—		—
Middleton Charles, miller, ditto	—	—	
Mudd Matthew, victualler, ditto			—
Nield Clement, bricklayer, ditto	—	—	
Offell William, millwright, Welney			—
Plumtree John, farmer, Upwell			—
Pooley William, yeoman, ditto			—
Poory Thomas, ditto, ditto			—
Reed John, victualler, ditto			—
Rowell John, schoolmaster, ditto			—
Rust William, farmer, ditto			—
Sanders John, ditto, ditto	—	—	
Smart Robert, ditto, ditto			—
Saffery Henry, clerk, ditto	—	—	
Scott Gabriel, tailor, ditto			—
Sedgeley John, farmer, ditto		—	—
Shepherd Thomas, sadler, ditto			—
Singleterry William, yeoman, ditto			—
Smith George, ditto, ditto			—
Turner John, farmer, ditto			—
Turner Robert, ditto, ditto			—
Turner John, ditto, ditto			—
Watton William, yeoman, ditto			—
West Thomas, farmer, ditto			—
Whitehead John, ditto, ditto	—	—	
Wilkinson Edward, ditto, ditto			—
Wakefield William, tailor, ditto		—	—
Wool Hugh, farmer, ditto			—
Wool Thomas, ditto, ditto			—

Upwell.—Freebridge Hundred.

	Win.	Coke	Wod.
Wright Thomas, farmer, Upwell			
Wool Robert, ditto, ditto	15	16	53.

Waborne.

	Win.	Coke	Wod.
Bolding William, farmer, Waborne			
Hammond Robert, bricklayer, ditto			
Nurse Edmund, farmer, ditto	3	3	0

Wacton.

	Win.	Coke	Wod.
Clarke John, gent. Wacton			
Copsie John, farmer, ditto			
Sallows John, ditto, ditto	2	2	1

Walcot.

	Win.	Coke	Wod.
Bacon William, farmer, Honing			
Baldwin Thomas, ditto, Walcot			
Cook Samuel, ditto, ditto			
Gaze John, ditto, ditto			
Harbord Robert, blacksmith, ditto			
Marler Robert, gent. ditto			
Warner William, ditto, ditto	0	0	7

Walpole St. Peter.

Bell John, farmer, Walpole St. Peter
Bransby Thomas, blacksmith, ditto
Capps Joseph, farmer, ditto
Carrell John, ditto, Terrington St. John
Creek Robert, wheelwright, Walpole St. Pet.
Cullen Christopher, farmer, ditto
Embling John, ditto, ditto
Fulwood Thomas, gamekeeper, ditto
Giddings William, farmer, Outwell
Hawes Joseph, ditto,
Harrison William, ditto, Walpole St. Peter
Ingram Robert, jun. ditto, ditto
Lowe John, ditto, ditto
Morphew John Cross, clerk, ditto
Newcome Charles, farmer, ditto
Newcome John, ditto, ditto
Newcome William, ditto, ditto
Pattern John, ditto, ditto
Pett John, ditto, ditto

Walpole St. Peter.

Smith Israel, farmer, Walpole St. Peter
Thistleton James, ditto, ditto
Thistleton John, ditto, ditto
Wood John, ditto, ditto

Walpole St. Andrew.

	Win.	Coke	Wod.
Boon Charles, farmer, Walpole St. Andrew			
Ingram Mallard, ditto, ditto			
Tweedy Robert, ditto, ditto			
Wade Jeremiah, publican, ditto			
Woodward John, farmer, ditto	12	11	12

Walsham North.

	Win.	Coke	Wod.
Ames Luke, carpenter, North Walsham	2	3	3
Angell William, farmer, ditto			
Aufrere George John, clerk, Ridlington			
Bond John, yeoman, Thurgarton			
Cooper Thomas, clerk, Loddon			
Cooper Thomas H. esq. North Walsham			
Chapman James, yeoman, ditto			
Colls Richard, shopkeeper, ditto			
Culley Richard, farmer, ditto			
Debenne Thomas, ditto, ditto			
Dobbs Daniel, bricklayer, ditto			
Dix Thomas, gent. ditto			
Draper John, wheelwright, ditto			
Debenne ——, shopkeeper, Trunch			
Dye James, tailor, North Walsham			
Forster William, gent. ditto			
Johnson Stephen, carpenter, Erpingham			
Hall William, butcher, North Walsham			
Hay Thomas, D. D. ditto			
Holmes John, farmer, Paston			
Hunter Henry, clerk, North Walsham			
Juler John, clock-maker, Swafield			
King Clement, farmer, Happisburgh			
Lacey John, farmer, North Walsham			
Le Neve William, baker. ditto			
Le Neve Charles, farmer, Moulton			
Leeds James, yeoman, North Walsham			
Legood James, innkeeper, Trunch			
Lloyd Thomas, clerk, North Walsham			

Walsham North.

	Win.	Coke	Wod.
Lane Groom, butcher, North Walsham			
Love Thomas, farmer, ditto			
Margetson John, ditto, ditto			
Payne John, jun. brewer, ditto			
Pilch John, farmer, ditto			
Pitcher William, miller, ditto			
Plumbly John, barber, ditto			
Powell William, farmer, ditto			
Reynolds John, clerk, Edinthorpe			
Robinson Richard, draper, East Ruston			
Sadler John, farmer, Clippesby			
Saul Richard, shoe-maker, North Walsham			
Shepperd William, merchant, ditto			
Steward John, cordwainer, East Ruston			
Woodrow Thomas, gent. Rollesby	18	15	31

Walsham South.

	Win.	Coke	Wod.
Cater Edmund, farmer, South Walsham			
Elliott John, ditto, ditto			
Ewels Francis, husbandman, Upton			
Fearman John, farmer, Chedgrave			
Grimson William, ditto, Thurton			
Jermyn James, blacksmith, South Walsham			
Littlewood William, farmer, ditto			
Marsh James, clerk, ditto			
Pratt James, glover, ditto			
Sibel John, farmer, ditto			
Smith James, waterman, ditto			
Steward Samuel, farmer, ditto	6	6	7

Walsingham Little.

Andrews Henry, barber, Little Walsingham
Backham James, wool-comber, ditto
Bircham Henry, cabinet-maker, ditto
Curtis James, gent. Little Walsingham
Drage William, auctioneer, East Dereham
England Richard, gent. Hindringham
Groom William, butcher, Little Walsingham
Groom John, gent. Burnham Westgate
Hague John, ditto, East Basham
Kittmer Benjamin, ditto, Little Walsingham
Lovick Samuel, auctioneer, ditto

Walsingham Little.

	Win.	Coke	Wod.
Minns John, baker, Little Walsingham			
Minns Lewis, miller, ditto			
Peach Paul, clerk, Great Snoring			
Playford Thomas, carpenter, North Basham			
Rix George, gent. Little Walsingham			
Rix William, ditto, Wells			
Rogester Richard, farmer, Little Walsingham			
Rush Richard, gent. ditto			
Scott William, farrier, ditto			
Theodorick Thomas, gent. Outwell			
Tilney William, carpenter, Little Walsing.			
Wedrill William, gent. ditto			
Yaxley Thomas, gardener, ditto			
Yaxley Matthew, gent. ditto	14	23	8

Walsingham Old.

	Win.	Coke	Wod.
Boon Jeremiah, farmer, Great Walsingham			
Brooke William, ditto, ditto			
Curll Samuel, ditto, ditto			
Tuck Robert, ditto, ditto			
Tuck George, yeoman, ditto			
Woodhouse Samuel, labourer, ditto			

Walsoken.

	Win.	Coke	Wod.
Anthony John, farmer, Walsoken			
Anthony John, jun. ditto, ditto			
Beakley John, ditto, ditto			
Bennington Robert, gardener, ditto			
Bull William, farmer, ditto			
Carter Richard, yeoman, ditto			
Cox John, farmer, ditto			
Catling John, ditto, ditto			
Climenson James, ditto, Upwell			
Dennis Joseph, butcher, King's Lynn			
Eburn Pitchers, gardener, Walsoken			
Foster Nathaniel, farmer, ditto			
Groome William, bricklayer, ditto			
Hawkins Daniel, farmer, ditto			
Hendry William, ditto, Grimstone			
Hudson John, gardener, Walsoken			
Kisbee John, farmer, ditto			
Knape William, ditto, ditto	4	6	2

Walsoken.

	Min.	Coke	Wod.
Knape Edward, farmer, Walsoken			
Lent Edward, ditto, ditto			
Legge William, ditto, ditto			
Long Henry, ditto, ditto			
Miles John, labourer, ditto			
Moss James, farmer, ditto			
Murley John, ditto, ditto			
Reynolds William, farrier, Terrington St. J.			
Sexton Richard, farmer, Walsoken			
Sharpe Stephen, ditto, ditto			
Southwell John, ditto, ditto			
Sutterby Daniel, ditto, ditto			
Sutton Francis, ditto, ditto			
Ward Robert, ditto, ditto			
Wing Robert, surgeon, ditto			
Willesee Dornall, farmer, ditto	19	20	20

Walton West.

	Min.	Coke	Wod.
Arton William, farmer, West Walton			
Ball William, ditto, Walsoken			
Bean Thomas, ditto, West Walton			
Bean William, ditto, ditto			
Bean William, jun. ditto, ditto			
Bonney John, ditto, ditto			
Dobbs John, miller, Walpole St. Peter			
Griffiths Thomas, labourer, West Walton			
Fisher John, farmer, ditto			
Fisher Thomas, ditto, ditto			
Hall Thomas, ditto, ditto			
Humphrey John, ditto, King's Lynn			
Hubbard Thomas, ditto, West Walton			
Lumpkin Nicholas, ditto, Walpole St. Peter			
Neal William, ditto, ditto			
Northwell John, ditto, Walsoken			
Stork William, ditto, West Walton			
Watts John, ditto, ditto			
Young Richard, ditto, Walsoken	7	8	12

Warham.

	Min.	Coke	Wod.
Blomfield John, farmer, Billingford			
Browne Samuel, ditto, Warham			
Hall Benjamin, publican, ditto			

U

Warham.

	Win.	Coke	Wod.
Houghton Edward, butcher, Wells			
Moore Thomas, farmer, Warham			
Parker Thomas, ditto, ditto			
Wenner H. Lang, B. D. Warham St. M.			
Whitaker Richard, carpenter, Wighton			
Wigmore James, wheelwright, Warham			
Wordingham William, farmer, Stifkey	10	10	0

Waterden.

	Win.	Coke	Wod.
Hill William Money, esq. Waterden			
Stibbard John, bailiff, East Rudham	2	2	0

Watlington.

	Win.	Coke	Wod.
Bennett Thomas, yeoman, Watlington			
Billing Edward, farmer, ditto			
Brofit John, cordwainer, ditto			
Burnham William, bricklayer, ditto			
Cardy Thomas, grocer, Middleton			
Chaplin Edward, clerk, Edgefield			
Codman John, farmer, Watlington			
Crisp Robert, victualler, ditto			
Dowsing William, gent. ditto			
Ducket Francis, farmer, ditto			
Harrison George, ditto, Caister St. Edmund			
Hurdleston John, yeoman, Watlington			
Page John, ditto, ditto			
Patrick Thomas, gent. ditto			
Porter John, ditto, ditto			
Sampson John, farmer, ditto			
Thompson Robert, schoolmaster, ditto			
Watson John, yeoman, West Winch			
Worrall John, farmer, Watlington			

Watton.

	Win.	Coke	Wod.
Barker Benjamin, esq. Watton			
Brett John, gent. ditto			
Baxton Robert, baker, ditto			
Dennis Robert, victualler, Great Ellingham			
Dorr Charles, farmer, ditto			
Francis Samuel, baker, Shipdham			
Frankland Henry, clerk, Barford			
Fletcher Henry, gent. Watton	18	18	1

Watton.

Name	Win.	Coke	Wod.
Fuller Samuel, farmer, Watton			
Grigson Edward Harvey, esq. Saham Toney			
Harvey Robert, ditto, Ovington			
Harvey John, ditto, Watton			
Hastings Smith, baker, ditto			
Hastings John, bricklayer, ditto			
Jerry Thomas, miller, ditto			
Lake Walter, hair-dresser, ditto			
Lincoln Thomas, farmer, ditto			
Lockett James, cooper, ditto			
Nott John, labourer, ditto			
Scott Thomas, clerk, ditto			
Starke Thomas, schoolmaster, L. Ellingham			
Stevens Edward, grocer, Attleborough			
Stebbing Thomas, carpenter, Watton			
Swallow Robert, surgeon, ditto			
Thompson William, farmer, Carbrooke			
Webster Henry, gent. Watton			
Younge Edward, grocer, Shipdham	3	4	24

Weasenham All Saints.

Name	Win.	Coke	Wod.
Campbell Charles, clerk, Weasenham			
Carr Thomas, miller, ditto All Saints			
Hall William, gelder, ditto			
Hotham Frederick, clerk, Burnham Ulph			
Leeds Stephen, farmer, Weasenham All St.			
Meek William, ditto, Stanhoe			
Purdy Thomas, ditto, Weasenham All St.			
Softly Thomas, husbandman, ditto	7	7	1

Weasenham St. Peter.

Name	Win.	Coke	Wod.
Gunton F. wheelwright, Weasenham St. P.			
Madwell Rose, gardener, ditto			
Sanctuary Thomas, farmer, ditto	3	3	0

Weeting.

Name	Win.	Coke	Wod.
Manning William, clerk, Weeting			
Pond Thomas, butcher, Deopham			
Willett Thomas, gent. Hingham	2	3	0

Welborne.

Name	Win.	Coke	Wod.
Green John, farmer, Welborne			
Porrett James, ditto, ditto	0	0	2

U 2

Wellingham.

Name	Win.	Coke	Wod.
Billing William, farmer, Weasenham St. P.			
Morecraft Thos. husbandman, Wellingham	2	2	0

Welney.

Name	Win.	Coke	Wod.
Amerson John, miller, Welney			
Baker Thomas, farmer, Upwell			
Beart Robert, ditto, Welney			
Bodger Abraham, ditto, ditto			
Gotobed John, ditto, ditto			
Hills John, ditto, Upwell			
Horn James, blacksmith, Welney			
Snelling Matthew, farmer, Upwell	2	2	6

Wells.

Name	Win.	Coke	Wod.
Atmer William, innkeeper, Yarmouth			
Bunn William, baker, Wells			
Bensly George, collar-maker, ditto			
Beckerton William, porter, ditto			
Bloom John, merchant, ditto			
Bloom James, ditto, ditto			
Brightmer James, glover, ditto			
Bouch Thomas, cutler, ditto			
Bottomley J. H. stone-mason, ditto			
Bloom Thomas, merchant, ditto			
Clarke Henry, carpenter, ditto			
Curson Matthew, mariner, ditto			
Canfer William, basket-maker, ditto			
Damant Guybon, surgeon, Coltishall			
Davy Samuel, schoolmaster, Wells			
Dennis Valentine, brewer, ditto			
Eaton Benjamin, gent. ditto			
Elvin John, hair-dresser, Wighton			
Elvin David, mariner, Wells			
Elvin William, jun. cordwainer, ditto			
Podder James, labourer, Burnham Overy			
Forster William, merchant, Wells			
Frost William, taylor, ditto			
Gibbs John, butcher, ditto			
Gardiner Francis, farmer, ditto			
Grove Henry, mariner, ditto			
Hall Robert, ditto, ditto			
Hammond William, butcher, ditto			

Wells.

	Win.	Coke	Wod.
Haycock John, merchant, Wells			
Harrison Thomas, ditto, ditto			
Haycock Robert, miller, ditto			
Hayhoe Thomas, mariner, ditto			
Haydon John, ditto, ditto			
Padley John, ditto, ditto			
Haycock Joseph, grocer, ditto			
Hill John, jun. esq. ditto			
Houghton Robert, butcher, ditto			
Hutson Peter, farmer, ditto			
Jickling Francis, sail-maker, ditto			
Isaac Nathaniel, tailor, ditto			
Leeder Robert, mariner, Great Snoring			
Legatt Samuel, cordwainer, Wells			
Long Matthew, ditto, ditto			
Magnus Richard, carpenter, ditto			
Morl Robert, mariner, ditto			
Mufft Henry, butcher, ditto			
Matsell John, confectioner, ditto			
Neal James, innkeeper, Briston			
Nettleton William, farmer, Wells			
Nettleton William, jun. merchant, ditto			
Oldman John, mariner, ditto			
Oldman Robert, fisherman, ditto			
Oxenborow Edward, merchant, ditto			
Parker Richard, shipbuilder, ditto			
Parker Samuel, mason, ditto			
Peace G. cordwainer, Burnham Westgate			
Proudfoot Robert, joiner, Wells			
Proudfoot Isaac, labourer, ditto			
Ransome William, wheelwright, ditto			
Race John, mariner, ditto			
Randall Matthew, blacksmith, Blakeney			
Rudd Isaac, farmer, Wells			
Sandys John, gent. ditto			
Seymons John, ditto, ditto			
Seal John, mariner, ditto			
Southgate Francis, grocer, ditto			
Smith Francis, ditto, ditto			
Stocking Thomas, innkeeper, ditto			
Tickell J. A. clerk, ditto			
Walker Henry, master mariner, ditto			

Wells.

	Win.	Coke	Wod.
Walker Benjamin, merchant, Wells			
Wells Matthew, farmer, ditto			
Webster John, schoolmaster, Yaxham			
Woodcock James, auctioneer, Wells			
Woods Henry, maltster, ditto			
Wright William, blacksmith, ditto			
Wright Thomas, gent. Langham	73	76	1

Wendling.

	Win.	Coke	Wod.
Allen John, farmer, Scarning			
Hopwood John, gardener, Wendling			
Jarvis Christopher, miller, East Dereham			
Moore Edmund, farmer, Beeston			
Page Edmund, ditto, Wendling			
Wiffin Jeremiah, ditto, Swanton Morley	3	5	3

Wereham.

	Win.	Coke	Wod.
Balls John, gent. King's Lynn			
Bull William, miller, Wereham			
Catton Robert, grocer, ditto			
Garrard John, farmer, ditto			
Hendry William, clerk, Boughton			
Houchen John, gent. Wereham			
Johnson Robert, farmer, ditto			
Robinson Hardy, clerk, Wretton			
Sewell Abraham, woolstapler, Wereham	6	6	3

Westacre.

	Win.	Coke	Wod.
Bunkell Henry, cordwainer, Stow Bedon			
Burrell Henry, farmer, Roydon			
Hamond Anthony, esq. Westacre			

Westfield.

	Win.	Coke	Wod.
Andrews John, farmer, East Dercham			
Stimpson Joseph, husbandman, ditto			
Vincent Samuel, farmer, Yaxham	3	3	0

Weston.

	Win.	Coke	Wod.
Andrews Stephen, farmer, Weston			
Andrews Michael, ditto, Great Witchingham			
Baker John, ditto, Weston			
Bidwell James, ditto, ditto	2	2	1

	Win.	Coke	Wod.

Weston.

Bidwell William, farmer, Weston
Custance William, ditto, Halvergate
Custance John, esq. Weston
Dell John, clerk, ditto
Emeris Robert, farmer, Limpenhoe
Foulger James, publican, Mundham
Girling John, farmer, Ringland
Hardy Charles, yeoman, Weston
Hardy James, bricklayer, Morton
Howlett William, farmer, Easton

| 3 | 3 | 11 |

Westwick.

Shepherd Christopher, farmer, Bradfield

| 0 | 0 | 1 |

Wheatacre All Saints.

Bond William, clerk, Wheatacre All Saints
Sayer Robert, miller, ditto
Tuttell William, farmer, ditto
Wrench William, ditto, ditto

| 2 | 2 | 2 |

Whinbergh.

Salter William, farmer, Hardingham
White Timothy, ditto, Garvestone

| 2 | 1 | 1 |

Whissonset.

Barker Stephen, farmer, Whissonsett
Bennett John, ditto, Saham Toney
Clarke James, husbandman, Whissonsett
Goggs Henry, farmer, ditto
Moulton Nathaniel, butcher, Worthing
Neale Thomas, carpenter, Whissonsett
Neale William, ditto, ditto
Parker Robert, blacksmith, ditto
Raven Nathaniel, grocer, ditto
Skinner William, farmer, ditto
Smith James, ditto, Horningtoft
White William, wheelwright, Whissonsett

| 11 | 12 | 1 |

Whitwell.

Ellis E. J. farmer, Kerdistone
Leeds John, gent. Whitwell

	Win.	Coke	Wod.

Whitwell.

Neal Henry, farmer, Whitwell
Parke Charles, ditto, ditto
Rodham Henry, ditto, ditto

| 1 | 4 | 4 |

Wicklhampton.

Sharman John, farmer, Wicklhampton
Smith Robert, ditto, Freethorpe

| 2 | 1 | 0 |

Wicklewood.

Bacon Thomas, husbandman, Wicklewood
Bales John, yeoman, ditto
Barnard George, farmer, Hackford
Cann James, husbandman, Wicklewood
Colman Rev. John, clerk, ditto
Dodd James, farmer, Shelfanger
Harper William, worstead weaver, Foulsham
Kirby Thomas, farmer, Wicklewood
Wrigglesworth William, ditto, Hackford

| 3 | 3 | 6 |

Wickmere.

Partridge Thomas, farmer, Briston

| 1 | 1 | 0 |

Wiggenhall St. Mary Magdalen.

Barton Wm. farmer, Wiggenhall St. M. M.
Buttrick Edmund, ditto, ditto
Castle George, ditto, ditto
Chilvers William, labourer, ditto
Frankland Jeffery, publican, ditto
Griggs Jacob, farmer, ditto
Gunton Thomas, ditto, ditto
Prolit Thomas, cordwainer, ditto
Sharpe William, farmer, Walsoken
Whisler Richd. ditto, Wiggenhall St. M. M.
Whisler John, ditto, ditto
Whisler Thomas, ditto, ditto
Wilkinson Nathaniel, yeoman, ditto
Youngs Richard, farmer, ditto

| 10 | 12 | 3 |

Wiggenhall St. Peter.

Hall John, farmer, Wiggenhall St. Peter
Woods Presgrave, ditto, ditto

| 2 | 2 | 0 |

Wiggenhall St. Germains.

	Win.	Coke	Wod.
Bentley James, carpenter, Wiggenhall St. G.			
Chad Edmund Haswick, gent. ditto			
Dasberry James, farmer, ditto			
Hait John, schoolmaster, King's Lynn			
Long James, baker, Wiggenhall St. Germ.			
Paven John, shopkeeper, ditto			
Taylor Thomas, blacksmith, ditto			
Watford William, innkeeper, King's Lynn			
Wilkinson Jere. cooper, Wiggen. St. Germ.			
Whistler William, farmer, ditto	10	10	0

Wiggenhall St. Mary the Virgin.

Buffham John, yeoman, Wig. St. Mary Vir.			
Buffham John, farmer, Wig. St. Germains			
Dennis William, gent. ditto			
Jewson Leonard, farmer, ditto	4	4	0

Wighton.

Brunton Thomas, carpenter, Wighton			
Cooper Blyford, currier, ditto			
Darby Robert, house-steward, ditto			
Judd Charles, butcher, ditto			
Plowright Edmund, farmer, Wood Norton			
Potter Thomas, ditto, Wighton			
Read Henry, ditto, ditto			
Reeve John, sen. ditto, ditto			
Rix W. L. ditto, ditto			
Secker Isaac, labourer, ditto			
Wright John, publican, ditto	11	11	0

Wilby.

Beevor George, clerk, Wilby			
Bowles Richard, farmer, Old Buckenham			
Palmer Richard, ditto, Wilby	1	2	2

Wimbotsham.

Garnham John, gent. Wimbotsham			
Raven Henry, farmer, Downham Market			
Royal Thomas, yeoman, Stow Bardolph			
Senkler John, farmer, Wimbotsham	3	3	1

X

Winch East.

	Win.	Coke	Wod.
Curl Richard, farmer, East Winch			
Foulkes James, clerk, Sutton			
Kent Edmund, gent. East Winch	2	2	1

Winch West.

Bennett Thomas, victualler, West Winch			
Browne Samuel, gent. King's Lynn			
Carter Richard, yeoman, West Winch			
Checker John, currier, ditto			
Moulton Noah, farmer, ditto			
Panton Thomas, ditto, Setchy			
Slapp William, butcher, West Winch	6	6	1

Winfarthing.

Algar William, gent. East Harling			
Briton Richard, farmer, Pulham St. Mary			
Coppin William, ditto, Winfarthing			
Doggett Daniel, ditto, Tibbenham			
Filby Edmund, ditto, Winfarthing			
Johnson Christopher, ditto, ditto			
Pilgrim Thomas, gent. ditto			
Woods Robert, farmer, ditto			
Wragg Thomas, ditto, ditto			

Winterton.

Bond Henry, miller, Winterton			
Davy John, husbandman, ditto			
Deary Robert, fisherman, ditto			
Green Robert, husbandman, Somerton			
Tubby John, shoe-maker, Hemsby			
Worts Richard, seaman, Yarmouth			
Wright John, husbandman, Winterton	8	8	1

Witchingham Great.

Blyth John, wheelwright, G. Witchingham			
Elmer John, farmer, ditto			
Foster P. Le Neve, merchant, ditto			
Howlett Benjamin, farmer, Bawdeswell			
Mills Paul, gent. Whissonset			
Moore Edward, farmer, Gt. Witchingham			
Palmer John, ditto, ditto			
Sewell Richard, ditto, ditto	1	1	6
	2	1	7

	Win.	Coke	Wod.

Witchingham Little.

Camplin William, publican, Acle — 0 0 1

Witlingham.

Walne William, gent. Pulham Market — 0 0 1

Witton.—Blofield Hundred.

Culley Robert, farmer, Witton
Whaites Charles, ditto, ditto — 0 0 2

Witton.—Tunstead Hundred.

Bullimore Joseph, farmer, Witton
Leggatt John, ditto, ditto
Turner John, ditto, Paston
Wodehouse the Hon. John, Witton — 0 0 4

Wiveton.

Blackwood Robert, farmer, Wiveton
Cooper Thomas, gardener, Little Snoring
Crofts Thomas, gent. Wiveton
Ramm James, brewer, Cley — 2 2 2

Woolverton.

Durrant Timothy, gent. King's Lynn
Jackson James, farmer, Darsingham — 1 1 1

Wood Norton.

Barwick John, farmer, Wood Norton
Fisher John, throwsterer, ditto
Fox Edward, farmer, ditto
Garratt Samuel, ditto, ditto
Gill W. B. gent. ditto
Sawyer Edmund, labourer, ditto
Skinner Matthew, clerk, ditto — 3 5 4

Wood Rising.

Darby Robert, farmer, Carbrooke
Wayland John, esq. Scoulton — 0 0 2

Woodton.

Beckwith Thomas, brick-maker, Bedingham
Brooks John, wheelwright, Woodton
Dann Robert, farmer, Topcroft

X 2

	Win.	Coke	Wod.

Woodton.

Gilbert Gershon, farmer, Woolton
Goose Cornelius, linen-weaver, ditto
Last Dring, farmer, Mulbarton
Matthews Richard, gent. Framingham Pigot
Suckling Robert, esq. Woodton
Warnoll Robert, farmer, Hempnall — 0 1 9

Wootton North.

Pickerell William, yeoman, North Wootton
Standbanks Heriot, farmer, Clenchwarton
Thompson William, ditto, North Wootton — 0 1 3

Wootton South.

Barber Thomas, gardener, King's Lynn
Chapman John, farmer, ditto
Curry Richard, ditto, South Wootton
Fungary Thomas, ditto, ditto — 4 4 0

Wormegay.

Barkham William, farmer, Wormegay
Bird John, ditto, ditto
Curties James P. ditto, ditto
Herbert C. P. gent. Outwell
Hogge Henry, esq. Wormegay — 4 5 1

Worstead.

Bane Richard, tailor, Worstead
Barnard Henry, schoolmaster, ditto
Bird William, gent. Newton St. Faith's
Brograve Sir George, bart. Worstead
Durrant John, blacksmith, Happisburgh
Goose William, dealer, Worstead
Hill Richard, shoe-maker, ditto
Postle William, farmer, Smallburgh
Springall Isaac, ditto, Morton
Shalders John, shopkeeper, Worstead
Stewart Charles, esq. ditto
Swan George, tailor, ditto
Tuck John, farmer, ditto
Tuck Robert, ditto, ditto
Warner William, yeoman, ditto
Wiseman Miles, farmer, ditto — 4 4 12

	Win.	Coke	Wod.

Worthing.
Blomfield Samuel, farmer, Swanton Morley
Blomfield Thomas, ditto, Worthing

(Worthing: Win. 2, Coke 2, Wod. 0)

Wortwell.
Bolton John, husbandman, Wortwell
Buxton Robert, blacksmith, ditto
Carver Robert, labourer, ditto
Crisp Samuel, surgeon, ditto
Drake Thomas, farmer, Mundham
Goodwin John, husbandman, Wortwell
Hardiman Archibald, farmer, ditto
Harvey Robert, ditto, Alburgh
Johnson James, ditto, Redenhall
Llewellyn Henry, clerk, Wortwell
Pheany Robert, farmer, ditto
Say Joshua, ditto, ditto

(Wortwell: Win. 4, Coke 4, Wod. 8)

Wramplingham.
Clare Fisher, farmer, Wramplingham
Farrow Robert, ditto, ditto
Gower George, miller, ditto
Nash Spooner, farmer, Sprowston

(Wramplingham: Win. 2, Coke 3, Wod. 2)

Wreningham.
Burton William, farmer, Wreningham
Burton Thomas, ditto, Forncet St. Peter
Day Matthew, ditto, Wreningham
Day Robert, ditto, ditto
Lane James, labourer, ditto
Long John, farmer, ditto
Long Benjamin, ditto, ditto

(Wreningham: Win. 2, Coke 3, Wod. 5)

Wretham West.
Windett Davy, farmer, Little Cressingham

(Wretham West: Win. 1, Coke 1, Wod. 0)

Wretton.
Bird Benjamin, yeoman, Wretton
Bowers William, ditto, ditto
Cooke Robert, farmer, ditto
Flatt Peter, ditto, ditto
Prick Robert, ditto, ditto
Taylor George, yeoman, ditto

	Wm.	Coke	Wod.

Wretton.
Townley William, yeoman, Stoke Ferry
Wright William, farmer, Castleacre

(Wretton: Wm. 5, Coke 6, Wod. 3)

Wroxham.
Buck John, merchant, North Lopham
Davey Charles, carpenter, Wroxham
Green Daniel, farmer, ditto
Green James, ditto, ditto
Howse John, esq. ditto
Humfrey John, clerk, Great Dunham
Preston Thomas, esq. Beeston St. Lawrence

(Wroxham: Wm. 2, Coke 4, Wod. 5)

Wymondham.
Anderson William, gent. Wymondham
Anderson Thomas, farmer, ditto
Austin Peter, butcher, ditto
Basey John, farmer, ditto
Boulton Edmund, miller, ditto
Bougen Philip, carpenter, ditto
Burrell John, farmer, ditto
Browne William, gent. ditto
Burroughs Randall, esq. ditto
Cann J. S. brewer, ditto
Coggle Matthew, butcher, ditto
Culpit William, carpenter, ditto
Culpit William, jun. ditto, ditto
Carter John Grime, farmer, ditto
Child John, cooper, ditto
Cooper Charles, glazier, ditto
Cook William, surveyor of roads, ditto
Daniel William, attorney, Wicklewood
Darell John, esq. Wymondham
Eagling Joseph, farmer, ditto
Foulsham James, hair-dresser, ditto
Fawcett William, clerk, ditto
Fulcher William, farmer, ditto
Graver G. Denny, gent. Little Barningham
Gooch Manning, gent. Larling
Goodwin William, farmer, Forncet St. Peter
Goldsmith Ambrose, ditto, Wramplingham
Gowell Robert, carpenter, Wymondham
Halls Thomas, glazier, ditto

Wymondham.

	Win.	Coke	Wod.
Harvey Robert, baker, Wymondham			
Harvey William, farmer, ditto			
Harvey William, brewer, ditto			
Harvey Samuel, felmonger, ditto			
Harvey George, gent. ditto			
Holman Thomas, sadler, ditto			
Howlett James, farmer, ditto			
Hubbard William, wheelwright, ditto			
Humphreys James, cordwainer, ditto			
Howlett Harcourt, farmer, ditto			
Jackson Charles, husbandman, ditto			
Jackson William, gent, ditto			
Kemp Richard, smith, ditto			
King William, butcher, ditto			
Large James, watch-maker, ditto			
Lain William, blacksmith, ditto			
Laws John, husbandman, ditto			
Leeder Thomas, farmer, Barford			
Lucas Jacob, baker, Wymondham			
Mace Thomas, farmer, ditto			
Matthews Robert, ditto, ditto			
Mitchell William, attorney, ditto			
Norton Edmund, ironmonger, ditto			
Oakley Thomas, farmer, Attleborough			
Palmer John, ditto, Morley St. Peter			
Pilgrim Thomas, ditto, New Buckenham			
Page Thomas, sen. gent. Wymondham			
Papillon William, clerk, ditto			
Parsons James, farmer, ditto			
Parsons Samuel, ditto, ditto			
Parker Jehosaphat, ditto, ditto			
Parke Jeremiah, shopkeeper, Hingham			
Ransome Gamaliel, attorney, Wymondham			
Reeve Owen, weaver, ditto			
Reynolds Francis, farmer, ditto			
Reynolds Philip, ditto, ditto			
Reynolds Zaccheus, weaver, ditto			
Saunders James, farmer, ditto			
Sheldrake John, tailor, ditto			
Sharpe James, carpenter, ditto			
Skipper David, farmer, ditto			
Stafford Thomas, grocer, ditto			

Wymondham.

	Win.	Coke	Wod.
Stannard John, wool-comber, Wymondham			
Syder John, brandy-merchant, ditto			
Syder John Haylett, gent. ditto			
Smith Matthew, ditto, Bunwell			
Smith Edmund, ditto, Wymondham			
Smith William, farmer, ditto			
Staff Samuel, baker, ditto			
Taylor John, farmer, ditto			
Tillett John, gent. ditto			
Turner John, farmer, ditto			
Watts John, bricklayer, ditto			
White Thomas, ditto, ditto			
Wiseman Edmund, weaver, ditto			
Woods James, baker, ditto			
	22	42	64

Yarmouth.

	Win.	Coke	Wod.
Absolon William, merchant, Yarmouth			
Adams James, gent. ditto			
Agnew Alexander, tailor, ditto			
Ainge Joseph, gent. ditto			
Algar Robert, ditto, ditto			
Allen Richard, miller, ditto			
Aldred John, silversmith, ditto			
Aldred Samuel Higham, haberdasher, ditto			
Amis Samuel, shipwright, ditto			
Andrews Robert, labourer, ditto			
Appleton Robert, ditto, ditto			
Ashley Jacob, carpenter, ditto			
Atkins John, carter, ditto			
Ayres William, ditto, ditto			
Ayton Ormesby, ditto, ditto			
Amis John, corn-meter, ditto			
Austin William, carpenter, ditto			
Austin Henry, auctioneer, ditto			
August William, carpenter, ditto			
Banyard James, schoolmaster, ditto			
Batley John, grocer, ditto			
Barnes John, publican, ditto			
Barker Samuel, grocer, ditto			
Baldry Francis, brazier, ditto			
Barnes William, shipwright, ditto			
Barrett Henry, captain, ditto			

Barnes Robert, cooper, Yarmouth
Barth William, merchant, ditto
Baldry George, carter, ditto
Barrett Joseph B. basket-maker, ditto
Barber William, draper, ditto
Bathis John, shipwright, Great Plumstead
Barton Esau, gent. Yarmouth
Barrett John, labourer, ditto
Barber Ezra, shopkeeper, ditto
Bateman Thomas, surgeon, ditto
Barber Samuel, lime-burner, ditto
Bales James, hair-dresser, ditto
Barnard Benjamin, carpenter, ditto
Barcham William, ditto, ditto
Bailey James Martin, cordwainer, ditto
Barker Samuel, esq. ditto
Barrett Thomas, boat-builder, ditto
Barnaby John, carter, ditto
Barber Robert, blacksmith, ditto
Barrett Randall, seaman, ditto
Bailey Joseph, cordwainer, ditto
Banyard Samuel, schoolmaster, ditto
Banyard Robert, butcher, ditto
Baker William, cordwainer, ditto
Bassey James, merchant, ditto
Ball John, tailor, ditto
Bensley Francis, cordwainer, ditto
Beales William, fisherman, ditto
Bennett John, linen-weaver, ditto
Betts Samuel, waterman, ditto
Bell Charles, mariner, ditto
Bensley James, ditto, ditto
Beckett Thomas, cordwainer, ditto
Beckett William Draper, brewer, ditto
Beckham Zeb. grocer, ditto
Bell Samuel, esq. ditto
Benson Thomas, cordwainer, ditto
Beart John, printer, ditto
Beckett John, carter, ditto
Bell Samuel, cornmeter, ditto
Bishop Thomas, liquor-merchant, ditto
Bishop Thomas, mariner, ditto

Y

Bircham Samuel, labourer, Yarmouth
Blomfield William, mariner, ditto
Blyth Thomas, seaman, ditto
Borrett Giles, surgeon, ditto
Boardman Richard M. baker, ditto
Bolter Joseph, ditto, ditto
Boulter Joseph, gent. ditto
Boulter John, captain, ditto
Boult James, mariner, ditto
Bowles Thomas, labourer, ditto
Bowles William, rope-maker, ditto
Bowles Samuel, mariner, ditto
Bowles Edward, ditto, ditto
Browne Benjamin, grocer, ditto
Browne William, gent. ditto
Browne John, ditto, ditto
Brewer Thomas, miller, ditto
Brewer John, carpenter, ditto
Bradbear Samuel, mariner, ditto
Browne Philip, bricklayer, ditto
Bryant Thomas, sailor, ditto
Brady William, carpenter, ditto
Brady William, painter, ditto
Bransby Isaac, cooper, ditto
Bradfield James, broker, ditto
Bracey John, bricklayer, ditto
Brooks Frederick, butcher, ditto
Brazell William, merchant, ditto
Brooks William, mariner, ditto
Bream Samuel, gent. ditto
Bream Samuel, jun. cabinet-maker, ditto
Breeze William, hair-dresser, ditto
Brown John, merchant, ditto
Brown Joseph, cordwainer, ditto
Browne Robert, grocer, ditto
Browne Charles, innkeeper, ditto
Bristow Nathaniel, seaman, ditto
Brooks Robert, yeoman, ditto
Breeze John, carpenter, ditto
Bunfellow John, tailor, ditto
Burton Charles, ditto, ditto
Bull James, mast-maker, ditto

Yarmouth.

	Win.	Coke	Wod.
Bititude Samuel, gent. Yarmouth			
Bulman John, corn-chandler, ditto			
Burton Robert Ferrier, gent. ditto			
Butler Jeremiah, bricklayer, ditto			
Burrage John, ditto, ditto			
Calf William, mariner, ditto			
Carrington Thomas, gent. ditto			
Callow William, meter, ditto			
Capon Robert, ditto, ditto			
Callow John, wine-cooper, ditto			
Carter Thomas, mariner, ditto			
Carr Thomas, ditto, ditto			
Carter Robert, ship-master, ditto			
Calver James, gent. ditto			
Carr Walter, seaman, ditto			
Chapman William, labourer, ditto			
Church William, mariner, ditto			
Chettleburgh James, gent. ditto			
Christmas John, seaman, ditto			
Christmas John, schoolmaster, ditto			
Chaplin John, gent. ditto			
Clements Valentine, cabinet-maker, ditto			
Clarke John, whitesmith, ditto			
Clifton Robert, gent. ditto			
Clarke John, grocer, ditto			
Clarke Levy Barlow, stationer, ditto			
Clarke William, victualler, ditto			
Clarke William, miller, ditto			
Collins John, cordwainer, ditto			
Cook John, ship-master, ditto			
Colls John, miller, ditto			
Coleman Edmund, seaman, ditto			
Coleby Dover, merchant, ditto			
Conyers James, mariner, ditto			
Comnesby William, blacksmith, ditto			
Cowell John, shipwright, ditto			
Collens John, carter, ditto			
Copeland Henry, seaman, ditto			
Cobb Simon, currier, ditto			
Cowell Thomas, publican, ditto			
Colman Matthew, linen-draper, ditto			
Cox Joseph, seaman, ditto			

Y 2

Yarmouth.

	Win.	Coke	Wod.
Cory Robert, esq. Yarmouth			
Cooper John, carpenter, ditto			
Cochrane Robert, mariner, ditto			
Colby John, whitesmith, ditto			
Cooper Samuel Lovick, clerk, Ingoldesthorpe			
Cox Thomas, publican, Yarmouth			
Cobb John, shoe-maker, ditto			
Corp Charles, mast-maker, ditto			
Cozens John, labourer, ditto			
Cook George, publican, ditto			
Crisp William, seaman, ditto			
Crabtree Edward, gent. ditto			
Craske Robert, baker, ditto			
Crowther Samuel, gent. ditto			
Crickmay Thomas, ship-master, ditto			
Crow Charles, cabinet-maker, ditto			
Crisp Thomas, mariner, ditto			
Crowfoot Charles, carter, ditto			
Crow William, chair-maker, ditto			
Crow William, cabinet-maker, ditto			
Cutlove John, glazier, ditto			
Cubitt Robert, plumber, ditto			
Day James, shipwright, South Walsham			
Dawson Samuel, baker, Yarmouth			
Davy Daniel, carpenter, ditto			
Dawson Henry, carter, ditto			
Davis William, labourer, ditto			
Davy Francis, porter, ditto			
Davy Robert, gardener, ditto			
Darnell Thomas, captain, ditto			
Diver William, liquor-merchant, ditto			
Downes William, surgeon, ditto			
Downing Henry, carpenter, ditto			
Downing James, broker, ditto			
Douglas John Lewis, shipwright, ditto			
Draper William, pilot, ditto			
Drury Cornelius, carpenter, ditto			
Durrant Robert Boult, confectioner, ditto			
Dacker James, mariner, ditto			
Dunkin Alexander, seaman, ditto			
Durrant Robert, bricklayer, ditto			
Dublack Thomas Annis, seaman, ditto			

Yarmouth.

Name	Win.	Coke	Wod.
Durrant Edward, yeoman, Yarmouth			
Dye Robert, cordwainer, ditto			
Dye Robert, caulker, ditto			
Dyball John, tailor, ditto			
Eastaugh Benjamin, boatman, ditto			
Ebbs Thomas, baker, ditto			
Ellard John, hair-dresser, ditto			
Elder Charles, carpenter, Denton			
Eldridge Wm. Nathaniel, gent. Yarmouth			
Eller Joseph, joiner, ditto			
Ellis Robert, labourer, ditto			
Ellis Thomas, victualler, ditto			
Elliot George, labourer, ditto			
Emms Samuel, gent. ditto			
Emms David, joiner, ditto			
English Isaac, labourer, ditto			
Ellard John, jun. grocer, ditto			
Errington George, rope-maker, ditto			
Ellis John Abigail, butcher, ditto			
Evans William, boatman, ditto			
Ferrier Richard, shopkeeper, Hemsby			
Farrow Thomas, tailor, Yarmouth			
Farrow William, breeches-maker, ditto			
Ferrett John, seaman, ditto			
Fisher James, esq. ditto			
Fickling Benjamin, ditto, ditto			
Fiddy Thomas, currier, ditto			
Fisher John, esq. ditto			
Fish James, cordwainer, ditto			
Flatman Robert, carpenter, ditto			
Fletcher John, captain, ditto			
Fleet Daniel, cabinet-maker, ditto			
Fox William, gent. ditto			
Forder William, cooper, ditto			
Foster Jeremiah, baker, ditto			
Fox Thomas, carpenter, ditto			
Forster Pexall, printer, ditto			
Forster John, clerk, Tunstead			
Fromow Samuel, baker, Yarmouth			
Fryer Thomas, wheelwright, ditto			
Francis William, porter, ditto			
Freeman John Ibrooke, grocer, ditto			

Yarmouth.

Name	Win.	Coke	Wod.
French Joseph, carter, Yarmouth			
Fulcher James, labourer, ditto			
Furnace William, seaman, ditto			
Garson John, carpenter, ditto			
Garwood John, ironmonger, ditto			
Garwood Thomas Fryer, plumber, ditto			
Garwood Thomas, gent. ditto			
George Samuel, sawyer, ditto			
Gilham Jonathan, confectioner, ditto			
Gilham Jonathan, jun. ditto, ditto			
Gill William, coach-maker, ditto			
Gillett Thomas, sail-maker, ditto			
Giles William, spinner, ditto			
Gillings Daniel, rope-maker, ditto			
Gilby John, sail-maker, ditto			
Girdlestone Thomas, M. D. ditto			
Glaspoole Henry, ironmonger, ditto			
Glover John, yeoman, ditto			
Gould William, esq. ditto			
Gourlay David, cordwainer, ditto			
Goffin Mathew, ditto, ditto			
Goodear Thomas, shoe-maker, ditto			
Goodings Thomas, twine-spinner, ditto			
Godfrey James, turner, ditto			
Goodwin John, caulker, ditto			
Gooch Thomas, labourer, ditto			
Goddard Godfrey, whitesmith, ditto			
Grudgefield Philip Scott, butcher, ditto			
Graves William, sail-maker, ditto			
Graves William, jun. ditto, ditto			
Greenwood Benjamin, schoolmaster, ditto			
Green John, carpenter, ditto			
Grapes Jonah, sail-maker, ditto			
Green James, waterman, ditto			
Grimble Phineas, pilot, ditto			
Greenwood Jonas, coach-maker, ditto			
Groom William, carpenter, ditto			
Gunton Gabriel, merchant, ditto			
Guyton Philip, cordwainer, ditto			
Gymer Thomas, cordwainer, ditto			
Harper Robert, labourer, ditto			
Haw Joseph, rope-maker, ditto			

Yarmouth.

Name	Win.	Coke	Wod.
Harris Robert, seaman, Sharrington			
Hall John, ditto, Yarmouth			
Hatton William, seaman, ditto			
Hall Stephen, twine-spinner, ditto			
Hammond Edward, shipwright, ditto			
Hammond Richard, jun. merchant, ditto			
Hammond Thomas, miller, ditto			
Hacon James, baker, ditto			
Harley C. Girling, gent. ditto			
Hammond William, bricklayer, ditto			
Hall Richard, carter, ditto			
Hammond Richard, merchant, ditto			
Harper Richard, ditto, ditto			
Hare Jacob, gent. ditto			
Hardy John, butcher, ditto			
Harrison Matthew, carpenter, ditto			
Harnton Benjamin, gardener, ditto			
Harrison William, grocer, ditto			
Halfpenny Bernard, gent. ditto			
Hall William, baker, ditto			
Harrison William, grocer, ditto			
Harvey Robert, carpenter, ditto			
Harrell William, shipwright, ditto			
Healy William, carpenter, ditto			
Hewitt John, sawyer, ditto			
Heasdale Benjamin, mariner, ditto			
Hindry Robert, shopkeeper, ditto			
Higham John Ward, glazier, ditto			
Hensby Thomas, gardener, ditto			
Hickling Robert, carter, ditto			
Hicks James, cabinet-maker, ditto			
Hodge William, fisherman, ditto			
Hook Daniel, pilot, ditto			
Hogarth David, tailor, ditto			
Holmes James, seaman, ditto			
Hooper William, shipwright, ditto			
Howlett John, labourer, ditto			
Holt William, ship-owner, ditto			
Holyoak William, musician, ditto			
Holmes Thomas, mariner, ditto			
Holmes Thomas, jun. cordwainer, ditto			
Horn John, gent. ditto			

Yarmouth.

Name	Win.	Coke	Wod.
Hovell Edward, gent. Yarmouth			
Hodgkinson Randall, carpenter, ditto			
Howes Thomas, ditto, ditto			
Hunt George, tailor, ditto			
Hunt Abraham, watch-maker, ditto			
Hurry William, merchant, ditto			
Hurry James, ditto, ditto			
Hurry William John, gent. ditto			
Hunt Nathaniel, hair-dresser, ditto			
Hubbard Daniel, mariner, ditto			
Hubbard John, bricklayer, ditto			
Hubbard Thomas, merchant, ditto			
Hubbard William, butcher, ditto			
Hunt Thomas, gent. ditto			
Hunt James, seaman, ditto			
Hunt John, smith, ditto			
Humfrey William, seaman, ditto			
Huke William, carpenter, ditto			
Jay William, gent. Runham			
Jackson James, cordwainer, Yarmouth			
Jay Charles, gent. ditto			
Jenny William, brewer, Acle			
Jermyn James, corn-chandler, Yarmouth			
Jex James, rope-maker, ditto			
Johnson Charles, innkeeper, ditto			
Johnson Samuel, shipwright, ditto			
Johnson James, mariner, ditto			
Johnson John, fisherman, ditto			
Johnson Robert, ditto, ditto			
Johnson William, ditto, ditto			
Juby Edmund, seaman, ditto			
Kendle Thomas, woollen-draper, ditto			
Kett Thomas, rope-maker, ditto			
Kerrison William, bricklayer, ditto			
Kemp John, gent. ditto			
Kemp Richard, cabinet-maker			
Kemp Richard, gardener, ditto			
Kent Meadow, coachman, ditto			
King Joseph, baker, ditto			
King Thomas, gaoler, ditto			
King Henry, baker, ditto			
King Samuel, ditto, ditto			

Yarmouth.

Name	Win.	Coke	Wod.
Knowles Henry, carter, Yarmouth			
Knowles Richard, sawyer, ditto			
Knights William, butcher, Filby			
Lacon Sir Edmund, knight, Filby			
Lark James, carpenter, Yarmouth			
Ladell Edward, gent. Bradiston			
Lawes James, merchant, Yarmouth			
Language Robert, cordwainer, ditto			
Larter John, carpenter, ditto			
Lamb James, watch-maker, ditto			
Lamb Robert, ditto, ditto			
Last William, sadler, ditto			
Last William, jun. ditto, ditto			
Lacon John, esq. ditto			
Larlham William, coach-master, ditto			
Larter Samuel, sawyer, ditto			
Lamb William, mariner, ditto			
Larke William, lieutenant R. N. ditto			
Lee Thomas, brewer, ditto			
Leggatt Thomas, broker, ditto			
Lewis Samuel, gent. ditto			
Lettis John, rope-maker, ditto			
Lettis Thomas, ditto, ditto			
Libbis John, ship-owner, ditto			
Lincoln Henry, tailor, ditto			
Libbis William, broker, ditto			
London John, wheelwright, ditto			
Lowrie Robert, draper, ditto			
London William, cordwainer, ditto			
Lovewell James, shipwright, ditto			
Lores William, gent. ditto			
Lonsdale Richard, glazier, ditto			
Lowne Benjamin, confectioner, ditto			
Loveridge Henry, carter, ditto			
Lock Henry, gardener, ditto			
Lucas George, clerk, Catfield			
Lucas Gibson, ditto, Yarmouth			
Luff Thomas, gent. ditto			
Manners William, mariner, ditto			
Marshall Benjamin, brazier, ditto			
Marshall John, carter, ditto			
Manship Thomas, seaman, ditto			

z

Yarmouth.

Name	Win.	Coke	Wod.
Macdonald Nicholas, seaman, Yarmouth			
Marshall Michael, mariner, ditto			
Martins James, cordwainer, ditto			
Mabson Rous, pilot, ditto			
May John, baker, ditto			
Martins Robert, carter, ditto			
Mack James, cordwainer, ditto			
Marjoram William, baker, ditto			
Mays William, tallow chandler, ditto			
Mallett James, sawyer, ditto			
Manby George Wm. barrack-master, ditto			
Metcalf Joseph, seaman, ditto			
Meal James, ditto, ditto			
Meek Robert, millwright, ditto			
Miles Elias, shipmaster, ditto			
Miller Thomas, cordwainer, ditto			
Miller Richard, jun. timber merchant			
Miller Robert, parish clerk, ditto			
Mickleburgh Robert, plumber, ditto			
Minter Samuel, labourer, ditto			
Mitchell Page, carpenter, ditto			
Miller Richard, gent. ditto			
Miller Richard, jun. solicitor, ditto			
Morley James, carter, ditto			
Morley Joseph, ditto, ditto			
Morgan Eli William, grocer, ditto			
Moore Samuel, whitesmith, ditto			
Moore Thomas, cordwainer, ditto			
Morter Thomas, whitesmith, ditto			
Moxon John, gent. ditto			
Moore Joseph, breeches-maker, ditto			
Morling Daniel, grocer, ditto			
Mundford Benjamin, labourer, ditto			
Naylor Thomas, seaman, ditto			
Nash Abraham, grocer, ditto			
Newson James, gardener, ditto			
Neave Thomas, rope-maker, Filby			
Newton George, shipwright, ditto			
Newhall Thomas, caulker, ditto			
Neale William, accountant, ditto			
Newhouse Robert, breeches-maker, ditto			
Nightingale Robert, pastry-cook, ditto			

Yarmouth.

Win | Coke | Wod.

Nightingale Charles, labourer, Yarmouth
Nichols John, seaman, ditto
Nichols James, shipwright, ditto
Nichols Thomas, sailor, ditto
Nichols William, cordwainer, ditto
Nicholson Nathaniel, ditto, ditto
Nichols Charles, schoolmaster, ditto
Newton Robert, carter, ditto
Nollorth Samuel, sawyer, ditto
Norfor William, carpenter, ditto
Nollorth Vincent, cordwainer, ditto
Norton Thomas, millwright, ditto
Norton John, mast-maker, ditto
Norfor William, rope-maker, ditto
Nobbs John, ship-carpenter, ditto
Nolborow Matthew, baker, ditto
Nollorth Joseph, cordwainer, ditto
Nuthall William, draper, ditto
Oakes John, grocer, ditto
Olley John, salesman, ditto
Oliver Joseph, labourer, ditto
Orfeur Thomas, seaman, ditto
Osborne Thomas, ditto, ditto
Otey John, mariner, ditto
Paget Samuel, jun. esq. ditto
Patterson James, hair-dresser, ditto
Payne Peter, gent. ditto
Page John, carter, ditto
Parker Thomas, sawyer, ditto
Parker Thomas, baker, ditto
Parker Nicholas, cordwainer, ditto
Paul Bennett, mast-maker, ditto
Palmer James, merchant, ditto
Palmer John, carter, ditto
Palmer Nathaniel, esq. ditto
Palmer William Danby, merchant, ditto
Palmer John Danby, ditto, ditto
Palmer William Danby, jun. ditto
Palmer William, gent. ditto
Paston William, waterman, ditto
Page Charles, maltster, ditto
Page Robert, bricklayer, ditto

Z 2

Yarmouth.

Wm. | Coke | Wod.

Pearson Edward, miller, Yarmouth
Penrice Thomas, esq. ditto
Peel Samuel, baker, ditto
Petrie John, pilot, ditto
Peck Wales, broker, ditto
Peake Thomas, cooper, ditto
Philips Stacey, sail-maker, ditto
Philips Robert, whitesmith, ditto
Pikeling John, jun. shopkeeper, ditto
Pigg Joseph, shipwright, ditto
Pickers Thomas, cordwainer, ditto
Pitts James, gent. ditto
Pickers Thomas, shipwright, ditto
Pigeon Nicholas, ditto, ditto
Pilis William, publican, ditto
Playford John, grocer, ditto
Plowman John G. mariner, ditto
Plummer John, carpenter, ditto
Plummer William, mariner, ditto
Plummer Francis, wheelwright, ditto
Prick John, gent. ditto
Proctor Richard, plumber, ditto
Preston Daniel, cordwainer, ditto
Preston Isaac, jun. esq. ditto
Prior William, husbandman, ditto
Preston Edmund, esq. ditto
Prior Francis, carter, ditto
Proctor Francis, sawyer, ditto
Purdy William, brewer, ditto
Purdy William, ship caulker, ditto
Pycraft Timothy, carpenter, ditto
Quinton John, shipwright, ditto
Ranney John Freame, solicitor, ditto
Reeve William, whitesmith, ditto
Reeve Valentine, waterman, ditto
Reynolds Francis Riddell, esq. ditto
Riches William, whitesmith, ditto
Riddlesdale Robert, corn-merchant, ditto
Rix Thomas, tailor, ditto
Riches Thomas, cordwainer, ditto
Rickaby William, yeoman, ditto
Richmond William, cordwainer, ditto

Yarmouth.

Name	Win.	Coke	Wod.
Robinson John, carpenter, Yarmouth			
Robinson James, seaman, ditto			
Robinson Samuel, grocer, ditto			
Rolfe John, carpenter, ditto			
Royall Paul, dyer, ditto			
Rockwood Brown John, grocer, ditto			
Rushmere Samuel, cordwainer, ditto			
Rudd John, turner, ditto			
Rudd Peter, lath-render, ditto			
Ruxby Thomas, cooper, ditto			
Sawyer John, ditto, ditto			
Sancroft James, surgeon, ditto			
Saunders William, merchant, ditto			
Sayers James, esq. ditto			
Sayers John, ditto, ditto			
Savage Samuel, cordwainer, ditto			
Savory William, butcher, ditto			
Scottow Richard, carpenter, ditto			
Scott Robert, kiddier, ditto			
Scott Gould, fisherman, ditto			
Scott James, baker, ditto			
Scottow William, ditto, ditto			
Sewell John, cutler, ditto			
Searum Robert, mast-maker, ditto			
Sewell William, grocer, ditto			
Seago William, hair-dresser, ditto			
Sexton William, game-keeper, ditto			
Seaman Thomas, publican, ditto			
Seaman John, bookseller, ditto			
Secker John, draper, North Walsham			
Shreeve William, gent. Yarmouth			
Shreeve William, ditto, ditto			
Sharpe Joseph, ditto, ditto			
Shelley John, gent. ditto			
Shelley John, jun. merchant, ditto			
Sherrington William, plumber, ditto			
Shepherd William, carter, ditto			
Sherrington Samuel, whitesmith, ditto			
Short John, cordwainer, ditto			
Silver John, carpenter, ditto			
Simmons Edmund, ditto, ditto			
Simpson William, cordwainer, ditto			

Yarmouth.

Name	Win.	Coke	Wod.
Simpson Richard, watch-maker, Yarmouth			
Simms Thomas, labourer, ditto			
Simpson Samuel, draper, ditto			
Skinner James, bricklayer, ditto			
Skoyles Thomas, glazier, ditto			
Slipper John, miller, ditto			
Sloman James, rope-maker, ditto			
Sloman Charles, baker, ditto			
Smith John, cordwainer, ditto			
Smith Thomas, gent. ditto			
Smith John, schoolmaster, ditto			
Smith Samuel, ditto, ditto			
Smith John, cordwainer, ditto			
Smith Robert, blacksmith, ditto			
Smith William, salesman, ditto			
Smith Robert Cooper, bricklayer, ditto			
Smith John, labourer, ditto			
Smith Simon, merchant, ditto			
Smith Robert, cooper, ditto			
Smallpage William, shipwright, ditto			
Smith William, surgeon, ditto			
Smeaton John, patten-maker, ditto			
Sparke James, ironfounder, Wendling			
Soanes William, rope-maker, Yarmouth			
Spilman John, ditto, ditto			
Spilman William, grocer, ditto			
Spauls James, labourer, ditto			
Steward William, esq. ditto			
Steward Timothy, esq. ditto			
Stokes John, ship-master, ditto			
Stolworthy David, gent. ditto			
Stolworthy Thomas, millwright, ditto			
Stanford William, watch-maker, ditto			
Starlee Nicholas, hair-dresser, ditto			
Stratton Robert, gent. ditto			
Stanford Joseph, glazier, ditto			
Stoddart Joseph, shipwright, ditto			
Stone William, gent. ditto			
Starling Joseph, hatter, ditto			
Story James, fish-curer, ditto			
Stevenson Jonathan, twine-spinner, ditto			
Stevenson Samuel, ditto, ditto			

Yarmouth.

	Win.	Coke	Wod.
Stevenson Isaac, cordwainer, Yarmouth			
Steel William, haberdasher, ditto			
Sutton Thomas, surveyor, ditto			
Swaine Joseph, cordwainer, ditto			
Swift Richard, watch-maker, Coltishall			
Swann James, cooper, Yarmouth			
Symonds William, hair-dresser, ditto			
Symonds Robert, gent. ditto			
Symonds Nathaniel, plumber, ditto			
Taylor James, carpenter, ditto			
Taylor William, surgeon, ditto			
Taylor John, shipwright, ditto			
Tenant Robert, sawyer, ditto			
Thompson John, druggist, ditto			
Thurrell Thomas, mariner, ditto			
Thomas John George, linen-draper, ditto			
Thomlinson John, chinaman, ditto			
Tilson Richard, bricklayer, ditto			
Tolme David, merchant, ditto			
Tolver Samuel, solicitor, ditto			
Tompson John, mariner, ditto			
Townshend Robert, carpenter, ditto			
Towers Richard, bricklayer, ditto			
Toll Henry, gent. ditto			
Tompson James, gent. ditto			
Tompson Simon, brazier, ditto			
Todd James, gent. ditto			
Tooke Edward, labourer, ditto			
Tomlinson Richard, chinaman, ditto			
Tooley William, carter, ditto			
Tooky Edmund, bricklayer, ditto			
Trett John, publican, ditto			
Tuckfield Thomas, hatter, ditto			
Turner Richard, clerk, ditto			
Tubby Henry, plumber, ditto			
Turner Dawson, esq. ditto			
Tyrrell John, cabinet-maker, ditto			
Vincent Henry, labourer, ditto			
Urquhart William, mariner, ditto			
Utting Samuel, upholder, ditto			
Watson Thomas, gent. ditto			
Ward John, publican, ditto			

Yarmouth.

	Win.	Coke	Wod.
Waters Mark, merchant, Stokesby			
Wacey John, maltster, Yarmouth			
Warrent William, cordwainer, ditto			
Watson John, esq. ditto			
Watts John, labourer, ditto			
Watts John, ditto, ditto			
Ward Philip, tailor, ditto			
Watson Benjamin, sail-maker, ditto			
Warren John, carpenter, ditto			
Warren James, mariner, ditto			
Walbank Richard, tailor, ditto			
Wade William, mariner, ditto			
Ward Thomas, baker, ditto			
Walford William, clerk, ditto			
Webster John, servant, ditto			
Wells Robert, yeoman, ditto			
Webb Thomas, mariner, ditto			
Welch William, tailor, ditto			
Weston Mark Munns, gent. ditto			
Wells George, waterman, ditto			
West Nathaniel, gent. ditto			
Webster Hammond, grocer, ditto			
Whiten William, yeoman, ditto			
Wigg Henry, plumber, ditto			
Wigg Lilly, shopkeeper, ditto			
Williams Michael, sailor, ditto			
Wilson Isaac, mariner, ditto			
Wilkerson John, labourer, ditto			
Wigg Robert, publican, ditto			
Williams John Hanbury, merchant, ditto			
Wooden Francis, jun. shipwright, ditto			
Woolsey John, merchant, ditto			
Wolverton Nicholas, cooper, ditto			
Woolsey Thomas, seaman, ditto			
Vorts William, baker, ditto			
Worship Harry Verelst, attorney, ditto			
Woodward Robert, carter, ditto			
Woolby William, fish-curer, ditto			
Woolsey Joseph, fisherman, Bradfield			
Wright William D. plasterer, Erpingham			
Yates Andrew, ship-owner, Yarmouth			
Yallop James, sawyer, ditto			
Youngs John, chaise-driver, ditto			
	423	436	301

Beccles.—Suffolk.

	Wm.	Coke	Wod.

Creed Samuel M. esq. Yarmouth
Dykes Philip, esq. Roydon
Girdlestone John Long, clerk, Swainsthorpe
Geoch John, usher, Gillingham St. Mary
Hunter William, gent. Thurton
Killett John, gent. Gildestone
Lidstone S. merchant, Gillingham St. M.
Libbis William, glazier, Chedgrave
Pean John, clerk, Roughton
Smith Jeremiah, attorney, Holt
Tiptod William, merchant, Hardiscoe
Welch W. whitesmith, Framingham Pigot

Benacre.
Gooch Sir Thomas, bart. Saxlingham

Blundeston.
Glasspoole John, farmer, Aldeby

Blyford.
Dresser John, farmer, Caister

Botesdale.
Barnes Robert, labourer, Pulham Market
Hepworth William, clerk, Sloely
Meadows Philip, gent. East Harling

Brandon.
Leech John, plumber and glazier, Feltwell
Wright George, clerk, Mundford

Bradwell.
Crowe Robert, farmer, Acle
Crowe John, farmer, Halvergate
Russell William, husbandman, Rollesby

Brendall.
Wegg William, schoolmaster, Upton

Broome.
Negus Francis Colman, clerk, G. Ellingham
Shorting Henry, M. D. Wood-dalling
Tayleure Samuel, clerk, Freuze
Plowman Thomas, farmer, Roydon

Bungay.
Barnes Isaac, merchant, Barham
Bohun J. F. B. clerk, Hardwick
Brightley James, blacksmith, Mendham
Burtsall Nelson, farmer, Ditchingham
Butcher Robert, ditto, ditto

Yarham:

	Wm.	Coke	Wod.

Cock Joseph, husbandman, Yarham
Fulcher Solomon, farmer, ditto
Hayhoe Charles, ditto, ditto
Hayhoe James, ditto, ditto
Holman Francis, thatcher, ditto
Pitcher Kirk, farmer, Little Brand
Rix Robert, ditto, Wicklewood
Royall Robert, ditto, Carleton Rode
Vincent John, yeoman, Bassingham

| | 3 | 5 | 6 |

Yelverton.
Barker Peter, farmer, Tharston
Chapman Matthew, brick-maker, Yelverton
Day Jeremiah Ives, clerk, ditto.

| | 2 | 2 | 1 |

SUFFOLK.

Alderton.
FRANK Richard, D. D. Shelton

Aldborough.
Raymond Burham, surgeon, Foulden

Bardwell.
Roper Robert, farmer, East Harling

Barton Great.
Cooper Thomas, clerk, Billingford

Barnham:
Davey William, gent. Thetford

Barton Mills.
Martin Edward Wenman, esq. Newton
Wale John, yeoman, Attleborough

Beccles.
Alexander Henry, major, Carbrooke
Blowers Edmund, watch-maker, Shotesham
Burrows Wm. school-master, Gillingham
Bohun George, gent. Toft Monks
Blowers Isaac, gent. Mendham
Carlos James, clerk, Thorpe

A a

Bingay.—Suffolk.

Cooper John, esq. Wymondham
Dreyer Richard, clerk, Thwaite
Forster Peter, clerk, Hedenham
Holmes Thomas, clerk, Woodton Rectory
Ives John; ditto, Yarmouth
Kerrison Matthew, esq. Ellingham
Lewes Woollian, surgeon, Hingham
Padlon Thomas, clerk, Bradfield
Prentice Samuel, grocer, Ditchingham
Reeve Thomas, clerk, Topcroft
Roberts George, cooper, Harleston
Scott John, tanner, Chedgrave
Shufflebottom Robert, minister, Broome
Symonds Samuel, blacksmith, Ditchingham

Bury.

Browne George, esq. Saham Toney
Chesson Isaac, innkeeper, Methwold
Greengrass John, cabinet-maker, Carbrooke
Harrison John, gent. Bressingham
Lanchester Robert, ditto, Rockland
Leathes George, esq. Reedham
Le Grice J. attorney, Wiggen. St. Mary Mag.
Leathes Geo. Reading, clerk, Wicklhampton
Leheup William Michael, esq. Diss
Mills Edward, clerk, Bintry
Robinson Henry, gent. Bressingham
Sams J. B. clerk, South Wootton
Scott James, innkeeper, Shimpling
Spencer John, servant, Feltwell

Coney Weston.

Bridgeman Edward, esq. Garboldisham

Corton.

Postle Robert, farmer, Yarmouth

Denham.

Pashley J. L. farmer, Denton

Elmham South, St. Margarets.

Freestone Anthony, esq. Rushall

Elmswell.

Clarke John, gent. Diss

Ellough.

Miles John, farmer, Attleborough

Eye.—Suffolk.

Cobbold John, brewer, New Buckenham
Fulcher John, labourer, Tivetshall St. Mary
Waythe Thomas, esq. Scole

Flixton.

Gower Thomas, farmer, Alburgh

Fornham.

Ord John, clerk, Burgh

Framsden.

List William, farmer, Diss

Framlingham.

Lee Charles, merchant, Diss

Glemham.

North Dudley, esq. Castleacre

Gorleston.

Amis Robert, blacksmith, Yarmouth
Bougen T. (South Town) merchant, ditto
Barnes Robert, clerk, Stanford
Blogg Samuel, (S. Town) sawyer, Yarmouth
Bell John Barker, merchant, ditto
Bunney James, carpenter, ditto
Cross William, esq. Caister
Gardener Wm. (S. Town) waiter, Yarmouth
Green James, merchant, ditto
Hindes Edward, farmer, Norton Subcorse
Holmes Francis, boat-builder, Yarmouth
Humphrey Henry, wheelwright, Rockland
Jay Samuel, captain, Yarmouth
Lacon Edmund Knowles, esq. ditto
Mickleburgh William, pilot, ditto
Murrell Robert, carpenter, Great Snoring
Preston Isaac, ship-builder, Yarmouth
Smith John, surgeon, East Ruston
Spence Matthew, innkeeper, Yarmouth
Tyler Wm. (South Town) merchant, ditto

Grundisburgh.

Dillingham Brampton Gurdon, esq. Letton

Halesworth.

Avarne Isaac, clerk, Bassingham
Cufaude John, attorney, Redenhall

Hemingston.

Leeds William, surgeon, Pulham Market

Herringfleet.—Suffolk.

	Win.	Coke	Wod.
Baker George, farmer, Acle			
Jenner George, ditto, Chedgrave			
Hinderclay.			
Bond Bernard, farmer, Roydon			
Hinton.			
Tacon Richard, farmer, Stockton			
Homersfield.			
Scales Samuel, gent. Alburgh			
Hoxne.			
Andrews William, farmer, Tivetshall St. M.			
Cook William, merchant, Mendham			
Clabburn John, farmer, Yarmouth			
Green William, schoolmaster, Pulham Mar.			
Hesilrigge Sir T. Maynard, bt. O.Buckenham			
Nobbs James, butler, Diss			
Pearl John, farmer, Shelton			
Press James, esq. Roydon			
Hunston.			
Ellis James, farmer, Thetford			
Ipswich.			
Browne William, architect, Yarmouth			
Coyte James, clerk, Cantley			
Drummond Thomas, clerk, Attleborough			
Edge John, clerk, Needham			
Eldred James, miller, Great Dunham			
Green Thomas, esq. Alburgh			
Moy William, postman, Scole			
Paston Edward, esq. Appleton			
Pinkney Valentine, glover, Northwold			
Steward Ambrose Harbord, gent. Yarmouth			
Tunney John Robert, clerk, Ditchingham			
Wallis Benjamin, clerk, Great Fransham			
Ixworth.			
Barsham James, gent. Fincham			
Wake Thomas, farmer, Dickleburgh			
Kessingland.			
Crowfoot John, farmer, East Bilney			
Meek Thomas, ditto, Loddon			
Skinner Owen, ditto, Hales			
Kesgrave.			
Cotton John, farmer, Bedingham			

Lakenheath.—Suffolk.

	Win.	Coke	Wod.
Gathercole Evans, farmer, King's Lynn			
Lawshall.			
Cowille Nathaniel, clerk, Walsoken			
Linstead.			
Kemp John F. farmer, Needham			
Lound.			
Morse Thomas, esq. Yarmouth			
Lowestoft.			
Arnold A. C. esq. Heckingham			
Cornaby Samuel, cooper, Langley			
Everard James, esq. King's Lynn			
Lockwood Richard, clerk, Potter Heigham			
Perkins Edmund, miller, Denton			
Ritson Bartholomew, clerk, Aldeby			
Skipper Edm. gent. Gillingham All Saint's			
Market Weston.			
Walne Thomas, gent. Redenhall			
Melford East.			
Nightingale Sir Charles, bart. Wereham			
Mettingham.			
Packard John, farmer, Ellingham			
Paul John Dawson, ditto, Toft Monks			
Smith John, ditto, Ellingham			
Micklefield.			
Brighton Wm. husbandman, S. Lopham			
Mildenhall.			
Orman Nathan, clerk, Wiggenhall St. Peter			
Mutford.			
Temple T. W. clerk, Wortwell			
Newmarket.			
Micklethwayt John, esq. Beeston St. And.			
North Boe.			
Boyden Robert, gent. Burgh St. Peter			
Farr John, esq. Hales			
Pakefield.			
Marston Robert, gent. Repps			
Pearce James, ditto, Yarmouth			
Pakenham.			
Bradfield B. farmer, Houghton le Hole			
St. Peter's.			
Alden Richard, farmer, Wortwell			

Redgrave.—*Suffolk.*

	Win.	Coke	Wod.

Wilson T. Admiral, Billingford
Ringsfield.
Postle Gunton, clerk, East Ruston
Rissby.
Leonard Robert, farmer, Hockwold
Roydon.
Ewen John Norris, clerk, Paston
Saxted.
Applewhite Adam, tailor, Harleston
Serham Parva.
Canham John, gent. Hilgay
Shadingfield.
Julians John, farmer, Surlingham
Sibton.
Rainbird Robert, farmer, Starston
Spink Robert, gent. ditto
Somerleyton.
Love John, clerk, Aldeby
Money Cammant. esq. Burgh St. Peter
Stanton.
Corsbie Joseph, gent. Ashwelthorpe
Stowmarket.
Browne Jabus, clerk, Yarmouth
Fisk Thomas, attorney, Pulham Market
Prentice Manning, draper, Burston
Stuston.
Clarke Robert, gent. ——
Sudbury.
Anson Frederick, clerk, Skeyton.
St. John's.
Brettingham Richard, gent. Weston
Webster John, farmer, Toft Monks
Thetford.
Wilkinson Joseph, clerk, Wretham
Uggeshall.
Barber Edmund, gent. Pulham Market
Undley.
Wardlaw Matthew, gent. Feltwell
Walberswick.
Wales Isaac, farmer, Denton

Walsham le Willows.—*Suffolk.*

	Win.	Coke	Wod.

Bullock John, farmer, Banham
Heigham John, clerk, Hackford
Walpole.
How John, farmer, Attleborough
Wattisfield.
Crabb Zachariah, gent. Diss
Welnetham Great.
Philips Robert, clerk, Kempstone
Wetheringset.
Bellman Rayner, clerk, Feltwell
Hardy William, farmer, Hempnall
Wenhaston.
Godfrey Thomas, farmer, Yarmouth
Westhall.
Baldry Charles, farmer, Yarmouth
Westleton.
Woods Alexander, farmer, Toft Monks
Weybread.
Barber John, farmer, Brockdish
Booty John, ditto, Banham
Burgess John, ditto, Brockdish
Carpenter Thomas, ditto, Yarmouth
Crickmore John, ditto, Brockdish
Eade Peter, clerk, Stow Bedon
Feaveryer David, miller, Needham
Fuller Richard, farmer, Banham
Wingfield.
Clarke John, labourer, Redenhall
Cotton John, farmer, Denton
Wortham.
Betts George, clerk, Blo Norton
Baldwin Henry, gent. Redenhall
Harrison Philip, ditto, Diss
Mullinger John, ditto, Blo Norton

Win.	Coke	Wod.
89	99	135

	Win.	Coke	Wod.
AMYOT Thomas, esq. East Carlton			
Andrews Jasper, carpenter, Cromer			
Atkinson John, brewer, Yarmouth			
Arnold John, gent. Little Walsingham			
Arnold Samuel, ditto, ditto			
Baker William, ditto, King's Lynn			
Baltis Matthew, cabinet-maker, G. Plumstead			
Battis James Limborough, dyer, ditto			
Barnard William, esq. Diss			
Beevor Chas. Inner Temple, esq. Hackford			
Beevor Edw. ditto, ditto, ditto			
Blogg Stephen, carpenter, Corpusty			
Browne Edward, esq. Swafield			
Brooke Henry, butcher, Bawdeswell			
Bunting Edward, merchant, Watton			
Bulman John, jun. carpenter, Yarmouth			
Card Edward, draper, Harleston			
Chappelow Leonard, clerk, Roydon			
Clayton Robert, warehouseman, Yarmouth			
Clarke James, gent. Aylmerton			
Clarke William, farrier, Wereham			
Collison Nicholas C. esq. Leziate			
Colman Samuel, clerk, Broome			
Colman Thos. Tawell, surgeon, Wicklewood			
Cooper J. attorney, Wymondham			
Crafer Thomas, esq. Roydon			
De Vere J. gent. Swannington			
Denman Thomas, M. D. West Winch			
Durrant William, esq. Scottow			
Fotherape Fran. haberdasher, King's Lynn			
Frere John H. esq. Roydon			
Godbee William, cordwainer, Attleborough			
Grand John, ditto, New Buckenham			
Greenwood Chas. coach-maker, Yarmouth			
Greenwood Jas. leather-cutter, ditto			
Harvey Charles, esq. Lingwood			

B B

	Win.	Coke	Wod.
Haw William, gent. Yarmouth			
Haines Thomas, tailor, ditto			
Hamerton Charles, paviour, Elsing			
Harbord Hon. Edward, esq. Southrepps			
Hasse Leig. barrister, Syderstrand			
Hamerton Thomas, paviour, Mattishall			
Hawkins Daniel, jun. oilman, Outwell			
Harvey John, carpenter, Fincham			
Hinchley John, ditto, Alburgh			
Horrex Edmund, esq. Foulden			
Hulton Henry, ditto, Tunstead			
Hunt John, gent. Rushall			
Ibbott Henry, ditto, Sporle			
Jones John, special pleader, Yarmouth			
Jones George, painter, ditto			
Joddrell R. P. esq. Saxlingham			
Ireson John, gent. West Bradenham			
Leeder Robert, esq. East Dereham			
Lens John, ditto, Hockham			
Lewis Nathaniel, leather-cutter, Yarmouth			
Long Leonard, gent. Forncet St. Peter			
Lubbock Sir John, bart. Lammas			
Lunn Robert, liquor-merchant, King's Lynn			
Mann John, calico-glazier, ditto			
Marsh Isaac, gent. Dickleburgh			
Margerum S. esq. Wymondham			
Marshall John, bricklayer, Yarmouth			
Massingham William Cawston, gent. Holt			
Nottingham Matthew, ditto, Downham			
Ogilvie George, esq. Swanington			
Page John, public clerk, Holt			
Pescott Chambers, cabinet-maker, K. Lynn			
Playford Henry, gent. Northrepps			
Pierson Robt. esq. Kerdiston			
Plestow John D. clerk, Watlington			
Plestow Thomas B. esq. ditto			
Poll Joshua, carpenter, Wymondham			
Quinton John, cabinet-maker, Yarmouth			
Roper Samuel, shoe-maker, Upwell			
Rudd William, carpenter, Downham			
Sayers James, gent. Yarmouth			
Shepperson Matthew, ditto, Flitcham			

London, &c.

	Win.	C.ke	Wod.

Smith Jonathan, tailor, Yarmouth
Stewardson Samuel, shipwright, ditto
Straycock James, mariner, ditto
Stracey George, esq. Rackheath
Sustenance Samuel, plumber, Caxton
Symonds Nat. Warner, merchant, Yarmouth
Tate Edmund, captain, ditto
Thurgar John, peruke-maker, Stody
Took John Baseley, esq. Tompson
Trowse Thomas, breeches-maker, Corpusty
Walpole the Rt. Hon. Lord H. Wickmere
Wallock William, merchant, Wereham
Wiseman Robert, victualler, Shimpling
Wooley Thomas, esq. Fordham
Worr James, butcher, Horsham St. Faith's

| | 68 | 71 | 94 |

DISTANT VOTERS.

ALDIS G. Littleport, Isle of Ely, surgeon, Wacton
Alington M. Swinhop, Linc. clk. Walsoken
Alroyd R. Tyald St. G. Camb. farmer, ditto
Allenby Geo. Holbeach, Lin. grazier, ditto
Anson Edward, Shuckburgh, esq. Buxton
Anson G. Colonel, esq. Hevingham
Askew Wm. Deptford, shipwright, K. Lynn
Ayre John, Wisbeach, gardener, Walsoken
Barnard S. Boston, Lincsh. gent. Welborne
Barnard Samuel, jun. ditto, ditto, ditto
Barnard William, ditto, ditto, ditto
Barber William, Beltam, farmer, Totts
Bannister Charles, Wisbeach, gent. Outwell
Bennett Edmund, Dungarron, in Ireland, lieutenant of royal navy, Yarmouth
Bellamy J. Wisbeach, attorney, W. Walton
Blackburn Gabey, Elm, farmer, Enneth

Distant Voters.

	Win.	Coke	Wor.

Bidwell T. St. Geo. Middlesex, gent. Caston
Borrett G. Southampton, farmer, Wortwell
Bowles John, Cambridge, surgeon, Corpusty
Bowis Thomas, Peterborough, gent. Hilgay
Brooke W. Lambeth, esq. Terrington St. C.
Brightwen J. Witham, Essex, gent. Diss
Browne C. jun. Leiston, clerk, Bio Norton
Broadbelt T. Cambridge, brewer, Thetford
Browne C. Harefield, carpenter, Wymondham
Browne James, Cambridge, clerk, Yarmouth
Brindley J. Rochester, Kent. ship-b. K. Lynn
Buckeridge R. Litchfield, clerk, Beighton
Burrows T. C. Landbeach, Cambsh. clerk, Wymondham
Burton Wm. Joseph, Chatteris, gent. Upwell
Casswall G. Lacomb Park, Herts. esq. Ormesby
Chalker C. Westborough, farmer, Redenhall
Chapman Benedict, ——, clerk, Claxton
Chester John, ——, farmer, Walsoken
Chester W. Merton Col. Ox. clk. Wood Rising
Clements Jos. Dover-Court, gent. Yarmouth
Climenson John, Ware, ditto, Upwell
Coke Edward, Longford, esq. Castleacre
Cross ——, Sandford, Linc. clerk, Hunstanton
Day Jere. C. Col. Camb. ditto, Deopham
Dawbarn R. B. Wisbeach, shopk. W. Walton
Dell Joseph, Coggeshall, gent. Brocklish
Deacon J. Leicester, jeweller, King's Lynn
DeHague G. Wilbraham, ——, clk. Aylsham
Denn R. Temsford, Bedf. gent. L. Dunham
Dixon David, Mitcham, ditto, Wereham
Edes J. Wisbeach St. Peter, esq. Emneth
Edwards Ed. Huntingdon, clerk, Syderstrand
Elwin M. Colchester, captain, Booton
Farish Wm. Cambridge, clerk, Starston
Fanshawe C. R. Dengay, Essex, ditto, Morton on the Hill
Fawssett T. Wisbeach, esq. Tilney All St.
Fenton John, Littleport, Camb. shepherd, Hockwold
Fitzjohn George, Baldock, gent. Setchy
Fitzjohn Robert, Hertford, brewer, ditto

Distant Voters.

Name	Win.	Coke	Wod.
Fitzjohn T. Wells, Hertford, brewer, Setchy			
Fitzjohn John, Stanmore, ditto, ditto			
Frusher W. Elm, Cambridge, farmer, Emneth			
Gaches J. Thorney, Camb. farmer, Walpole St. Peter			
Gibbs G. Peterborough, draper, Upwell			
Girdlestone J. Thorney, Isle of Ely, clerk, Walsoken			
Girdlestone Henry, Cambridge, gent. Wells			
Gordon J. Wisbeach, clothier, Walsoken			
Gower John Lewis. Bilhill, Berks. esq. Sporle			
Green J. Isleham, Camb. miller, Feltwell			
Graves Thos. Tidd St. Giles, ditto, farmer, West Walton			
Graves Townley R. Frittown, esq. Upwell			
Gutteridge Wm. Wisbeach, steward, Emneth			
Haighton R. Cambridge, clerk, Hapton			
Hales J. Turner, Hartingham, esq. Hemsby			
Hamerton Charles, Wansford, Northampton-shire, paper-maker, Lyng			
Hardwick R. Wisbeach, surgeon, Terring-ton St. Clement			
Hardmeat Joseph, ditto, butcher, Walsoken			
Harlock John, Ely, brewer, Upwell			
Hewitt George, Cambridge, clerk, Witton			
Herbert Nat. Vin. Biggleswade, Bedfordshire, merchant, Wiggenhall St. Mary Mag.			
Hendry N. Bennett Col. Cam. clk. Stanfield			
Herbert W. Huntingdon, gent. Castleacre			
Herbert Geo. Biggleswade, merchant, ditto			
Hill J. Wisbeach, watch-maker, Walsoken			
Hibbert John, Milton, gent. Hilgray			
Hobart C. H. Bere Ferris, Devonshire, clerk, Wymondham			
Howell Joseph, Market-street, Hertford, esq.			
Jackson Hugh, Wisbeach St. Peter, attorney, Walsoken			
Jecks Isaac, Wisbeach, merchant, W. Walton			
Jenyns G. L. Cambridge, clk. W. Dereham			
Jones Lewis, Ely, ditto, Kenninghall			
Jones T. L. Broughton, ditto, Brettingham			
Johnson John, Wisbeach, farmer, Walsoken			

Distant Voters.

Name	Win.	Coke	Wod.
Johnson William, Elm, gent. Upwell			
Johnson James, Wisbeach, ditto, Outwell			
Isaacson W. Landwade, farmer, Hilgay			
Kerrich Thomas, Cambridge, clerk, Denton			
Kent N. Fulham, Middlesex, gent. Marsham			
Kent Charles, ditto, esq. ditto			
Layton William, Ely, farmer, Yarmouth			
Larwood Josh. R. N. clerk, Swanton Morley			
Lee Robert, Wisbeach, gent. Walsoken			
Lewin R. H. March, brewer, Wiggenhall St. M.			
Leathes M. Muster, Kent, clk. Itteringham			
Life Thomas, _____, merchant, Outwell			
Lloyd J. M. Lancing, Sussex, esq. Eccles			
Lloyd John, Grimsthorpe, grazier, Wells			
Lloyd W. Eddenham, Linc. grocer, ditto			
Loveday Arthur, Oxford, clerk, Antingham			
Lucas Wm. C. C. C. Camb. _____, Sporle			
Mann William, Sileham, gent. Brockdish			
Marsh I. L. Cambridge, ditto, Brundall			
Marler Benjamin, Oakley, farmer, Gissing			
Marsh S. Cambridge, gent. Dickleburgh			
Matthews T. Wisbeach, ditto, Walsoken			
Martin Robert, Ely, esq. Hilgay			
Martin Henry, ditto, draper, Downham			
Metcalfe Charles, Wisbeach, gent. Walsoken			
Metcalfe William, Ely, clerk, Watlington			
Moon E. Fanningham, clerk, Baddingham			
Morphew J. Dover-Court, Essex, esq. Wal-soken			
Moore T. Elm, Cambridge, farmer, Emneth			
Morris J. Wisbeach St. Mary, ditto, Wal-pole Saint Peter			
Orton R. Upwell, Cambridge, farmer, Wig-genhall St. Mary M.			
Orsborne James, St. Ives, gent. Downham			
Parr S. Hatton, Warwickshire, D. D. Repps			
Partridge H. Barrack House, esq. Cranworth			
Palmer J. B. Quadring, Lincoln. grazier, Tilney St. Lawrence			
Page Thomas, Ely, esq. Southery			
Peckover Jonathan, banker, Walsoken			
Peyton Sir H. Bucknell, Oxford, bart. Emneth			

Distant Voters.

	Win.	Coke	Wod.
Preston George, Lexden, Essex, clerk; Briston			
Redin James, farmer, West Walton			
Richmond Benjamin, roper, Downham			
Ripshaw Joseph, Wisbeach, gent. Walsoken			
Roberts Charles, Braintree, esq. Boughton			
Routh Samuel, Magd. Coll. Oxford, clerk, Wicklewood			
Sebright Sir John, Beachwood, Herts, bart. Bridgham			
Skeepshanks Thomas, Wimpole, Camb. clk. Walsoken			
Shinfield Edward, Wisbeach, stay-maker, Terrington St. John			
Shepherd Thos. Grantham, Lincoln. farmer, Wells			
Shrewsbury Wm. Littleport, ditto, Welney			
Smith John, Erton, ditto, Hilgay			
Spalding J. Peterborough, surgeon, Outwell			
Stevens Stephen, Ely, clerk, Upwell			
Suckling Wm. Windsor, esq. Banham			
Taylor Mark, Littleport, farmer, Upwell			
Thurston J. Manhead, Devon. gent. Great Barwick			
Tokelove T. Doddington, shopkeeper, Upwell			
Tokelove John, ditto, grocer, ditto			
Torry Wm. Wisbeach, farmer, ditto			
Tyssen Sam. Canterbury, esq. Narborough			
Vipan Benj. ——, innkeeper, Walsoken			
Watson Wm. Wisbeach, brewer, ditto			
Walford Thomas, ditto, gent. ditto			
Walton M. Elm, Cambridge, farmer, Emneth			
Westwood James, Littleport, ditto, Welney			
Whiteman Henry; ——, gent. Upwell			
Whittaker Thos. Sylham, clerk, Mendham			
Wing John, Thorney, esq. Southery			
Wodelhouse.J.T. Cambridge, M.D. Gresham			
Worth John, Oakley, esq. Langmere			
Wodehouse E. Colchester, gent. G. Ryburgh			
Youngman John, Waterbeach, Cambridge. gent. Tivetshall St. Mary			
	89	101	71

COMPARATIVE VIEW OF THE PLUMPERS, GIVEN AT THE ELECTIONS OF 1802 AND 1806.

ALPHABETICAL LIST OF THE HUNDREDS AND BOROUGHS, WITH The Number of Votes for each Candidate.

	Win.	C.	Wod.
Blofield	70	73	31
Brothercross	71	71	4
Clackclose	218	230	86
Clavering	42	46	95
Depwade	61	91	117
Diss	104	129	86
Earsham	64	87	91
Erpingham North	129	112	62
Erpingham South	98	119	120
Eynsford	114	122	86
	Win.	Co.	Wo.
Flegg East	51	56	36
YARMOUTH	423	436	301
	474		
Flegg West	27	33	81
Forehoe	68	93	187
Freebridge Lynn	379	413	157
LYNN	115	127	91
	264	286	66
Freebridge Marshland	126	125	75
Gallow	70	77	26
Greenhoe North	153	190	84
Greenhoe South	37	59	93
Grimshoe	36	45	119
Guiltcross	52	72	96
Happing	49	55	113
Henstead	56	59	21
Holt	124	126	57
Humbleyard	22	32	45
Laundich	135	162	99
Loddon	53	60	69
Mitford	84	116	137
Shropham	152	143	156
THETFORD	107	89	101
	45	54	55
Smithdon	75	-83	15
Taverham	52	61	32
Tunstead	50	57	139
Walsham	57	62	73
Wayland	40	31	91
NORWICH	129	132	105
SUFFOLK	89	99	135
LONDON, WESTMINSTER, &c.	68	71	24
DISTANT VOTERS	89	101	71
	3722	4118	3365

COMPARATIVE VIEW OF THE PLUMPERS, GIVEN AT THE ELECTIONS OF 1802 AND 1806.

HUNDREDS.	In 1802. PLUMPERS.				In 1806. PLUMPERS.			
	Voters	A.	C.	W.	Voters	Wm.	C.	Wod.
Blofield	100	0	3	55	107	1	2	23
Brothercross	69	0	16	0	74	0	0	2
Clackclose	379	14	4	40	305	2	4	70
Clavering	145	0	1	105	134	1	3	81
Depwade	211	1	3	146	179	0	2	87
Diss	178	2	5	28	190	1	3	159
Earsham	145	1	6	73	155	1	3	66
Erpingham North	171	1	3	111	170	3	0	46
Erpingham South	243	1	5	102	197	3	2	78
Eynsford	240	4	6	57	177	2	1	161
Flegg East	845	3	2	398	786	7	5	238
Flegg West	110	0	1	82	107	0	3	70
Forehoe	273	0	6	65	253	2	2	152
Freebridge Lynn	474	10	3	20	536	0	9	113
Freebridge Marshland	195	2	0	7	193	4	2	50
Gallow	116	0	10	11	97	2	5	15
Greenhoe North	192	3	10	6	196	2	6	12
Greenhoe South	143	4	5	50	114	1	0	61
Grimshoe	159	0	0	57	156	0	3	109
Guiltcross	142	0	12	33	142	1	1	63
Happing	166	0	0	143	156	0	2	94
Henstead	74	0	4	29	74	0	0	14
Holt	216	13	1	34	177	1	1	40
Humbleyard	80	0	1	43	69	0	1	35
Laundich	222	0	11	47	225	1	1	57
Loddon	123	0	1	74	117	0	0	51
Mitford	246	1	11	106	264	1	4	106
Shropham	280	0	7	123	280	1	0	103
Smithdon	105	1	6	5	91	1	1	7
Taverham	89	1	4	34	84	1	1	23
Tunstead	179	2	2	146	182	0	1	117
Walsham	139	0	2	99	102	3	0	36
Wayland	129	0	1	88	120	4	1	73
Norwich	281	1	3	121	225	1	4	79
Suffolk	223	0	5	12	217	1	0	110
London, Westminster, &c.	63	3	-0	13	93	0	1	22
Distant Voters	109	2	2	20	160	1	4	54
	7253	70	160	2692	6904	54	76	2702
	3612	4317	3516		3722	4118	3365	

State of the Poll.....

AN INDEX,

Or List of the Towns in the County of Norfolk, divided into the Hundreds in which they lie, and the Page in which each Town is to be found.

OTHER TITLES AVAILABLE FROM
S.A. & M.J. RAYMOND
6 Russet Avenue, Exeter EX1 3QB

THE
SUFFOLK
POLL BOOK
1790

RAYMONDS ORIGINAL POLLBOOKS

MANY OTHER TITLES AVAILABLE
SEND SAE FOR FULL LIST